Eine Bildreise

Oskar Fehrenbach/Norbert Kustos/Ellert & Richter Verlag
Schwarzwald
The Black Forest/La Forêt-Noire

Oskar Fehrenbach
geb. 1923; Studium der Philosophie, Deutschen Literatur und Kunstgeschichte mit Promotion. Seit 1953 Arbeit als Journalist, zuletzt Chefredakteur der Stuttgarter Zeitung. Autor mehrerer Veröffentlichungen.

Norbert Kustos
geb. 1957 in Lahr; nach dem Studium der Germanistik und Geschichte intensive Beschäftigung mit der Fotografie; arbeitet als freischaffender Bildjournalist in Karlsruhe; Veröffentlichungen u. a. bei Geo-Frankreich, Globo, Saison, Zeit-Magazin sowie diversen Kalender-Publikationen.

Oskar Fehrenbach
born in 1923, studied philosophy, German literature and art history and took his PhD before embarking on a career in journalism in 1953, working latterly as editor-in-chief of the Stuttgarter Zeitung. He has written several books.

Norbert Kustos
born in Lahr in 1957, took up photography after reading German studies and history at university. He works as a freelance photographer in Karlsruhe. His work has appeared in Geo France, Globo, Saison, Zeit Magazin and a number of calendars.

Oskar Fehrenbach
Né en 1923; études de philosophie, de littérature allemande et d'histoire de l'art; doctorat. Journaliste depuis 1953 et, en dernier lieu, rédacteur en chef du Stuttgarter Zeitung. Auteur de plusieurs publications.

Norbert Kustos
Né en 1957 à Lahr. Après des études de germanistique et d'histoire, se consacre intensément à la photographie. Travaille comme photo-journaliste free-lance à Karlsruhe. Publications dans Géo-France, Globo, Saison, Zeit-Magazin et ouvrages divers sous forme de calendriers.

Titel/Cover/Titre:
Der Bollenhut, ein schönes Schmuckstück der Schwarzwälder Tracht.
The "Bollenhut," a crowning glory of the traditional Black Forest costume.
Le «Bollenhut», belle parure faisant partie du costume traditionnel de la Forêt-Noire.

Text und Bildlegenden/Text and captions/Text et légendes:
Oskar Fehrenbach, Simonswald
Fotos/Photos/Photographie:
Norbert Kustos, Karlsruhe
Übertragung ins Englische/English translation/Traduction anglaise:
Paul Bewicke, Hamburg
Übertragung ins Französische/French translation/Traduction française:
Michèle Schönfeldt, Hamburg
Karte/Map/Carte géographique:
ComputerKartographie Huber, München
Lektorat/Editor/Lectorat:
Iris Klein, Hamburg
Gestaltung/Design/Maquette:
Hartmut Brückner, Bremen
Satz/Typesetting/Composition:
KCS GmbH, Buchholz/Hamburg
Lithographie/Lithography/Lithographie:
ORT GmbH, Hamburg
Druck/Printers/Impression:
Ara-Druck GmbH, Stuttgart
Bindung/Binding/Reliure:
Großbuchbinderei Hollmann, Darmstadt

Die Deutsche Bibliothek —
CIP-Einheitsaufnahme

Schwarzwald = The Black Forest / Oskar Fehrenbach; Norbert Kustos. —
Hamburg: Ellert und Richter, 1993
(Eine Bildreise)
ISBN 3-89234-398-5
NE: Fehrenbach, Oskar; Kustos, Norbert; PT

Inhalt/Contents/Sommaire

Älter als die Alpen oder: der ungekrönte König unter den Mittelgebirgen

Wann ist er am schönsten? Im Frühjahr oder im Sommer? Im Herbst oder im Winter? — Aus dem Schwarzwald schallt das Echo zurück: Bei mir ist es immer schön, rund ums Jahr: im Mai, wenn die Wiesen mit bunten Blumen übersät sind, wenn die wilde Kirsche mitten unter Tannen blüht und die Natur ihr erstes großes Freudenfest feiert. Im August, wenn der Sommer in all seiner Pracht auf den Gipfeln leuchtet und der Wanderer unter dem Dach der Bäume Kühlung findet. Im Herbst, wenn die belaubten Wälder in allen Farben feurig funkeln, oder wenn an klaren Tagen über der Dunstglocke des Wolkenmeeres die Alpenkette bis ins Berner Oberland mit seinen Viertausendern zum Greifen nahe vor den Augen liegt. Oder im Winter gar, wenn die Tannenwipfel von einem weißen Schneekleid überzogen sind und die Eiskristalle im Licht der Wintersonne zu gleißen und zu glitzern beginnen. Du kannst es drehen und wenden, wie Du willst: Ich bin zu allen Jahreszeiten verlockend.

Zugegeben: Ich kann auch rauh und abweisend sein, wenn der Westwind durch die Burgundische Pforte hereinfegt, wenn er die Bäume zerzaust und die Nebelschwaden talaufwärts treibt, wenn die Blätter wirbeln und der Wind den Wanderer an die warme Stube denken läßt, die auf einem der alten Höfe, in einem Dorfgasthaus oder in einer Nobelherberge auf ihn wartet. Eines aber lasse Dir noch sagen: Wann immer Du mich aufsuchst, Du findest eine göttliche Ruhe bei mir. Hier kannst Du „abschalten" und endlich wieder einmal Frieden mit Dir selbst und der Natur schließen. Hier läßt sich die Hektik des Alltags vergessen, hier findest Du Stille, Einsamkeit und Gastlichkeit. Denn ich bin — und damit sei mein Eigenlob vollendet — der ungekrönte König unter den deutschen Mittelgebirgen.

Wer über den Schwarzwald schreibt, dem muß eine solche Huldigung erlaubt sein.

Dieses Gebirge, das sich über eine Länge von 150 Kilometern vom Oberrheinknie bis Pforzheim erstreckt, besitzt eine magische Ausstrahlung. Ihr kann sich keiner entziehen. Denn noch (die Betonung liegt vorsichtshalber auf dem Wörtchen „noch") ist es von unvergleichlicher Urwüchsigkeit. Nirgendwo sonst gibt es einen so harmonischen Dreiklang von Wald, Wiese und Wasser. Der Schwarzwald ist der Musterfall einer offenen, von Bäumen nicht vollkommen überwucherten Landschaft, die den Blick nicht verbaut, sondern in unendliche Weiten lockt. Das gilt vor allem für den südlichen Schwarzwald, der irgendwo zwischen Kinzigtal und Höllental beginnt, sich von dort über das Feldbergmassiv hinzieht und in Richtung Schweiz langsam abflacht. Es gab Zeiten, in denen die Viehweiden bis auf die Höhen hinaufreichten. Doch allmählich, mit dem Rückgang der Landwirtschaft, macht sich der Wald in manchen Gebirgsgegenden immer breiter und zieht den Bergen eine Kappe über den Kopf. Nicht so im Südschwarzwald. Da gibt es noch die kahlköpfigen Gipfel, die ihre markanten Konturen in den Horizont zeichnen. Und da sieht man dann auf den freien Flächen noch die alten Bergbauernhöfe, die sich in eine Mulde schmiegen und vollkommen mit der Landschaft verschmelzen. Eine Landschaft, die eben deshalb fasziniert, weil sie unverändert karg und herb ist, zugleich voller Lieblichkeit und Sanftheit in ihren weit ausladenden Schwingungen. Reichtum hat es hier nie gegeben, es sei denn in den großen Klöstern. Dagegen Armut, die vor hundertfünfzig Jahren noch viele außer Landes nach Amerika getrieben hat. Herr und Knecht, Bauer und Tagelöhner, waren getrennt. Mancher verdiente sein armseliges Brot als Glasbläser, als Köhler oder Harzer, der die Rinden anzapfte, um die begehrte Flüssigkeit zu gewinnen. Bis ins letzte Jahrhundert gab es ertragreiche Bergwerke, deren Stollen noch heute im Wald versteckt sind. Silber und Erz wurden gewonnen, doch längst lohnt sich die Schürfung in diesen unterirdischen Schatzkammern nicht mehr. Natürlich hat auch der Schwarzwald Anschluß an die industrielle Entwicklung gefunden. Wo früher die Tüftler das Wunderwerk der Kuckucksuhren an langen Winterabenden gebastelt und dann sommers in alle Welt getragen haben, werden die „glocks" heute fabrikmäßig hergestellt und mit vorgefertigten Schnitzereien versehen.

Diese bodenständige Tradition hat auch die Menschen geprägt. Sie sind ruhig, gelassen, manche etwas rauhbeinig, die meisten aber heiter und von hintersinnigem Humor. Es gibt nur wenige, die noch die Zipfelmütze über den Kopf ziehen, wenn ein „Fremder" kommt. An der Wende vom Winter zum

Older than the Alps or: The uncrowned king of the central mountain ranges

When is it at its loveliest? In spring or summer? In autumn or winter? The echo resounds from the Black Forest itself: I am always lovely, all year round: in May when the meadows are strewn with brightly coloured flowers, the wild cherry blossoms amidst the fir trees, and Nature holds her first great celebration. In August, when summer glows in all its splendour upon the mountain tops and the hiker finds cool shade beneath the canopy of leaves. In autumn when the forest foliage sparkles with a myriad of fiery colours, or on clear days when the Alps as far as the Bernese Oberland, with its 12,000-feet peaks towering out of the haze over a sea of clouds, seem almost near enough to touch. Or indeed in winter when the fir tree tops are draped in a white veil of snow and ice crystals begin to glisten and glitter in the light of the wintery sun. You can twist and turn whichever way you like: I am enticing in every season.

Admittedly, I can also be harsh and cold, when the West wind blows in through the Belfort Gap, ruffling the trees and driving the swathes of mist up the valley, when the leaves swirl and the hiker thinks of the warm room that awaits him in one of the old Black Forest houses, a village guest-house or a high-class inn. But let me tell you one thing: whenever you seek me out, in me you will always find divine stillness. Here you can "switch off" and once more at last find peace with yourself and Nature. Here you can forget the hustle and bustle of everyday life, here you will find quiet, solitude and hospitality. For—let this be the end of my paean of self-praise—I am the uncrowned king of the German central mountain ranges.

Anyone writing about the Black Forest must be allowed the indulgence of paying such homage. This mountain range, stretching 150 kilometres from the sharp bend in the Upper Rhine as far as Pforzheim, possesses a magical aura. Nobody can escape it. For it is still (as a precaution, the emphasis is on the word "still") a region of incomparably unspoiled nature. Nowhere else is there such a harmonious triad of forest, meadow and water. The Black Forest is the ideal example of an open landscape not entirely covered by trees, which instead of obstructing the gaze draws it into the infinite distance. This applies particularly to the southern part of the Black Forest, which starts somewhere

**Plus ancienne que les Alpes ou:
la reine sans couronne des montagnes
moyennes**

6/7

between Kinzigtal and Höllental, spreading from there across the Feldberg massif and gradually flattening out towards Switzerland. There were times when the cattle grazing meadows extended high up into the mountains. But gradually, with the decline of agriculture, the forest is spreading further and further over many mountain areas and covering the mountain tops. However, not in the southern Black Forest. Here there are still bare mountain tops, their striking contours drawn on the horizon. And here in the open spaces you can still see the old mountain farmsteads nestling in hollows and blending perfectly into the landscape. A landscape which fascinates precisely because of its blend of unremitting sparseness and severity mingled with the charm and gentleness of its sweeping undulations. This was never the home of wealth, except perhaps in the big monasteries. On the contrary, there was poverty, which 150 years ago drove many people overseas to America. Master and servant, farmer and wage-labourer were separated. Many earned a meagre living as glass-blowers, charcoal burners or by tapping tree bark to obtain the valuable resin. Up until the last century there were highly productive mines, their workings hidden in the forest still today. Silver and ore were extracted, but mining in these subterranean treasure vaults has long ceased to pay. Naturally the Black Forest has also become acquainted with industrial development. Whereas in former times craftsmen spent the long winter evenings chipping away at the intricate detail of the cuckoo clocks which they sold all over the world in summer, nowadays the clocks are factory-made and decorated with prefabricated carvings.

Long-established tradition has also shaped the character of the people. They are quiet, calm, many of them somewhat rough-and-ready, but most are cheerful and have a cryptic sense of humour. There are only a few who still pull their pointed caps down over their heads when a "stranger" comes. As winter turns to spring Black Forest dwellers in many places even turn into "madmen" when Fasching wreaks its havoc. This

Quand est-elle la plus belle? Au printemps ou en été? En automne ou en hiver? De la Forêt-Noire nous parvient l'écho: je suis belle tout au long de l'année. En mai, lorsque les prés sont constellés de fleurs multicolores, que les cerisiers sauvages fleurissent au beau milieu des sapins et que la nature célèbre dans l'allégresse sa première grande fête. En août, quand l'été resplendit sur les sommets dans toute sa magnificence et que le promeneur trouve la fraîcheur sous les frondaisons de mes arbres. A l'automne, lorsque le feuillage de mes forêts étincelle de ses feux incandescents ou que, par temps clair, la chaîne des Alpes, qui s'étend jusqu'à l'Oberland bernois et dont les sommets atteignent quatre mille mètres d'altitude, émerge de la cloche brumeuse de sa mer de nuages. En hiver même, lorsque la cîme de mes sapins est recouverte d'un blanc manteau et que les cristaux de glace se mettent à étinceler et à scintiller dans la lumière du soleil hivernal. Nul besoin de te torturer l'esprit plus longtemps: je suis envoûtante en chaque saison. Certes, je peux manquer de clémence et me montrer inhospitalière lorsque le vent, s'abat sur mes sommets après s'être engouffré par la Trouée de Belfort, qu'il ébouriffe les arbres et chasse les traînées de brouillard en remontant les vallées, que les feuilles tourbillonnent, faisant naître chez le promeneur le désir de se retrouver dans l'intérieur douillet d'une des vieilles fermes, d'une auberge de village ou d'une hostellerie de luxe. Mais il est une chose que tu dois savoir: quelle que soit la saison à laquelle tu me rendes visite, un calme divin t'attend chez moi. Tu pourras oublier tes soucis quotidiens, t'y réconcilier enfin avec toi-même et avec la nature. Tu oublieras l'agitation de la vie de tous les jours en même temps que tu y trouveras le silence, la solitude et l'hospitalité. En effet-et c'est ainsi que je mettrai fin à mon propre encensement —, je suis la reine sans couronne des montagnes de moyenne altitude. Qu'il soit permis à celui qui se propose d'écrire au sujet de la Forêt-Noire, de lui rendre un tel hommage. Une magie se dégage, en effet, de cette chaîne de montagnes qui s'étire sur une longueur de 150 kilomètres, du «Genou» que forme le cours supérieur du Rhin jusqu'à Pforzheim. Personne ne saurait y échapper. Car elle possède encore (l'accent est mis ici, par prudence, sur le petit mot «encore») un caratère naturel et rustique incomparable. Nulle part ailleurs n'existe une harmonie semblable à celle que forment les trois éléments que sont ici la forêt, les prairies et l'eau. La Forêt-Noire est un exemple de paysage «ouvert» que les arbres n'ont pas réussi à envahir totalement, un paysage qui ne masque pas la vue mais entraîne le regard du spectateur dans les

infinies profondeurs de l'horizon. Cela vaut tout particulièrement pour la partie sud de la Forêt-Noire qui commence quelque part entre Kinzigtal et Höllental, déploie ses massifs par-delà le Feldberg et perd lentement de l'altitude en approchant de la Suisse. Il fut un temps où les paturages grimpaient jusque sur les hauteurs. Cependant, le déclin de l'agriculture a entraîné, dans certaines régions, une prolifération sans cesse croissante de la forêt, qui recouvre désormais les sommets d'une calotte de verdure. Ceci n'est pas le cas, il est vrai, du sud de la Forêt-Noire. On y trouve encore des sommets chauves, projetant sur l'horizon les contours de leurs formes accusées. Ainsi peut-on apercevoir, sur les surfaces dégagées, les vieilles fermes de montagnes qui se tapissent au creux des vallons, se fondant entièrement au paysage. Un paysage dont la fascination émane de ce qu'il est demeuré aride et austère, en même temps qu'il est imprégné du charme et de la douceur des amples ondulations de son tracé de collines. La richesse n'y a jamais existé, sauf dans les grands monastères. Par contre, une telle pauvreté y régnait encore, il y a cent cinquante ans à peine, que nombre de ses habitants durent quitter le pays et prendre le chemin de l'Amérique. Maître et valet, fermier et journalier vivaient séparément. Certains gagnaient leur maigre pitance comme souffleurs de verre, charbonniers ou résiniers qui gemmaient l'écorce pour en recueillir le précieux liquide. Jusqu'au siècle dernier y ont existé des mines de haut rendement dont les galeries se dissimulent aujourd'hui encore au cœur de la forêt. L'argent et les minerais en étaient extraits, mais la prospection de ces sources de richesse souterraines a, depuis bien longtemps déjà, cessé d'être rentable. La Forêt-Noire a su s'adapter au progrès industriel. Alors que, jadis, les paysans, horlogers à leurs heures, bricolaient le merveilleux mécanisme des pendules à coucou, en hiver, à la veillée, afin de pouvoir les vendre un peu partout en été, les «glocks» sont aujourd'hui produits en série et ornés de sculptures sur bois préfabriquées.

Le terroir et sa tradition a également donné son empreinte aux habitants de la région. Ils sont de nature calme et pondérée, certains même assez rustres, mais la majorité est de caractère plutôt gai et douée d'un sens ambigu de l'humour. Rares sont aujourd'hui ceux qui se barricadent chez eux quand ils voient arriver un étranger au pays. Lorsque l'hiver fait place au printemps et que le

Älter als die Alpen oder:
der ungekrönte König
unter den Mittelgebirgen

Older than the Alps or:
The uncrowned king of the central
mountain ranges

Frühjahr werden die Schwarzwälder an manchen Orten sogar „närrisch", wenn die „Fasnet" ihr Unwesen treibt. Mit rheinischem Karneval hat dies nichts zu tun. Sie verstecken sich hinter Masken, werden zu Hexen und Glonkern, die tollen Mummenschanz mit ihren Mitmenschen treiben.

Wer etwas Witterung für den Charakter von Landschaften mitbringt, wird den Schwarzwald in sein Herz schließen. Er ist rundum bauchig, längst nicht so schroff und faltenreich wie die benachbarten Alpen, dafür jedoch erheblich älter, zurechtgehobelt in vielen Jahrmillionen. Die geologische Vergangenheit ist ehrwürdig, sie reicht zurück bis ins ältere Tertiär. Manches klingt fast wie eine Legende. Da, wo sich der Schwarzwald auf der rechten und die benachbarten Vogesen auf der linken Rheinseite wie zwei zum Verwechseln ähnliche Brüder gegenüberliegen, war in Urzeiten ein gewaltiges Grundgebirge. „In einem Zerrungsbereich der Erdkruste", wie es die Fachleute formulieren, hat sich ein „Grabenbruch" gebildet, so daß Vater Rhein bei Basel eine Kurve machen mußte, um sich den Weg in Richtung Nordsee zu bahnen. Darum fallen auch beide Gebirge zur oberrheinischen Tiefebene hin steil ab, zerfurcht von weiten Tälern und gesäumt von einzigartigen Städten. Freiburg, Straßburg, Basel, das ist im südwestdeutschen Länderdreieck ein Dreigestirn hochgetürmter gotischer Gotteshäuser, die ihresgleichen suchen. Diese „Regio", die sich europäisch verschwistert, ist Drehscheibe und Barriere zugleich. Im Süden grenzt der Schwarzwald an die Schweiz, im Osten an die Ausläufer der „Schwäbischen Alb", beziehungsweise an den Bodensee, im Westen an Frankreich. Auf seinen Höhenzügen berührt man unablässig die europäische Wasserscheide. Gelegentlich laufen die Quellwasser sogar parallel zueinander, das eine allerdings zum Rhein hinab, das andere in Richtung Donau. In der berühmten Wutachschlucht bei Neustadt/Bonndorf hätten sich Rhein und Donau beinahe die

Hand gereicht, doch dann hat der jugendhaft übermütige Rhein der noch dünn fließenden Donau das Wasser abgegraben, so daß die Wutach in grauer Vorzeit nicht den weiten Weg ins Schwarze Meer auf sich nahm, sondern sich „klamm-heimlich" dem Oberlauf des Rheins in die Arme warf.

Über die Zauber- und Verwirrspiele der Natur wird noch manches zu erzählen sein. Ebenso vielfältig und verwirrend ist die „Humangeschichte". Lassen wir sie nicht schon in der Steinzeit, sondern bei den Kelten beginnen, die als erste historisch „faßbar" sind. Spektakuläre Funde aus jüngster Zeit beweisen, daß schon die Kelten eine hohe Kultur besessen haben, die sich weit über den Raum nördlich der Alpen erstreckte. Noch vor der Zeitenwende jedoch kamen sie mit den Römern ins Gehege, wurden aufs Haupt geschlagen und schließlich während des dritten Jahrhunderts von den Alemannen überrollt. Die Alemannen ihrerseits, die sich selber Sueben (Schwaben) nannten, haben dann wieder die Römer vertrieben und sich bis heute behauptet. Les allemands, so nennen die Franzosen die Deutschen bis auf diesen Tag, was aber nichts daran ändert, daß sich „Alemannen" ebenso im Elsaß wie im Nordwestzipfel der Schweiz finden lassen. Geblieben ist vor allem auch die alemannische Mundart, die Johann Peter Hebel so wunderbar zum Klingen gebracht hat, daß ihn sogar der Dichterfürst Goethe mit Lob bedachte.

Längst jedoch haben die stammesgeschichtlichen Unterscheidungen an Bedeutung und Einfluß verloren. Politisch gehörte der Schwarzwald geraume Zeit zu Baden, einem Großherzogtum von Napoleons Gnaden, das bis nach Mannheim hinauf Pfälzer, Franken und Alemannen unter einem liberalen Dach vereinigte, ehe es nach dem Zweiten Weltkrieg die Bindestrich-Ehe mit Württemberg einging, so daß Stuttgart zur Hauptstadt des Südweststaates avancierte, während sich das verwaiste Karlsruhe als „Residenz des Rechts" bescheiden mußte. Hier müßte sich ein Kapitel über die dynastische Vorgeschichte anschließen, die jedoch wie überall im alten „teutschen Reich" auf die Schilderungen von Flickenteppichen hinausliefe. Um die wichtigsten „Herrschaften" zu nennen: Bis ins 12. Jahrhundert haben die Zähringer großartige Spuren hinterlassen, später gehörten die südlichen Landesregionen zu „Vorderösterreich", dann schließlich breitete das „Haus Baden" seine Fittiche übers ganze Land. Beim Besuch einiger Städte werden wir dann wieder auf die dynastischen Spuren stoßen. Im Schwarzwald aber, dabei bleibt es, regieren die Bäume.

has nothing to do with Carnival on the Rhine. They hide behind masks, disguised as witches and demons engaging in fantastic masquerades with their fellow-humans.

Those with a feel for landscape character will take the Black Forest to their hearts. It is nicely rounded, and far less steep and craggy than the neighbouring Alps, though considerably older, having been smoothed out over millions of years. Its geological provenance is a noble one, stretching back to the earlier tertiary period. Much about it sounds almost like the stuff of legends. The Black Forest on the right bank of the Rhine lies opposite the neighbouring Vosges on the left bank, like two brothers bearing a confusingly close resemblance to each other. Here in prehistoric times there was a mighty mountain chain. As the experts put it, "at a point of tension in the Earth's crust" a rift was formed, so that Old Father Rhine had to form a bend near Basle in order to clear himself a path to the North Sea. That is why both mountain ranges drop steeply towards the Upper Rhine lowland plain, which is furrowed by long valleys and lined with unique towns. The South West Triangle's Big Three, the steepled Gothic cathedrals of Freiburg, Strasbourg and Basle, are without compare. This region with its European sisters is at once a crossroads and a barrier. The Black Forest borders on Switzerland to the South, on the Schwäbische Alb and Lake Constance to the East and on France to the West. On its mountains one constantly comes across the European watershed. Here and there the spring waters flow parallel to each other, one going down to the Rhine and the other towards the Danube. In the famous Wutach Gorge near Neustadt/Bonndorf the Rhine and Danube were on the verge of shaking hands with each other, but then the Rhine in its youthful arrogance snatched away the sparsely flowing Danube's livelihood, and so in far off times the Wutach, instead of taking up the challenge of the path to the far-off Black Sea, flung itself secretly into the arms of the Rhine's upper reaches. There will be much to relate about the magical and tangled games of Nature. The history of human beings in this area is equally rich and tangled. Let's begin not with the Stone Age but with the Celts, the first people who can be "grasped" historically. Recent spectacular finds have demonstrated that the Celts possessed a refined culture which stretched far and wide across the area north of the Alps. However even in the

Plus ancienne que les Alpes ou:
la reine sans couronne des montagnes
moyennes

8/9

pre-Christian period they got in the way of the Romans, were defeated and finally overrun by the Alemannic tribes during the third century. In turn the Alemanni, who called themselves Suebi (Swabians), drove the Romans out again and have held their ground unto this day. Though still today the French call the Germans "les allemands" this does not alter the fact that there are Alemanni both in Alsace and in the north-west corner of Switzerland. What has survived above all is the Alemannic dialect, which the writer Johann Peter Hebel made to sound so harmonious that he even earned the praise of Goethe, prince of poets.

However, tribal distinctions have long since lost much of their significance and influence. For some time the Black Forest belonged to Baden, by the grace of Napoleon a Grand Principality, which united people from the Palatinate, Franconians and Alemanni under one liberal roof. After World War II it entered into its double-barrelled alliance with Württemberg, and Stuttgart advanced to become capital of the south-western state of Baden-Württemberg, whilst the abandoned Karlsruhe had to make do with being the seat of the Federal Supreme Court. Here one should really add a chapter about dynastic history, but like everywhere else in the ancient German empire it would end up being a patchwork description. To name the most important "lords and masters" up to the 12th century AD the Zähringer left an impressive legacy. Later the southern districts of the territory became part of Austria, and then finally the House of Baden spread its wings over the whole territory. We shall come upon dynastic traces again when paying visits to various towns. But one thing remains certain: in the Black Forest it is the trees which reign.

«Fasnet», le carnaval local, enfièvre les esprits, les habitants de certains endroits de la Forêt-Noire sont comme saisis de folie. Cela n'a d'ailleurs rien à voir avec le carnaval rhénan. Les gens du pays dissimulent leurs visages derrière des masques, se transformant en sorcières et en «Glonkern» qui entraînent leurs compagnons dans une mascarade endiablée.

Qui sait, tant soit peu, flairer le caractère propre à certaines régions, s'éprendra d'emblée de la Forêt-Noire. Elle est mamelonnée de toutes parts, bien moins plissée que les Alpes voisines, mais, par contre, beaucoup plus vieille et fut rabotée au cours des millions d'années de son existence. Son passé géologique, qui remonte au paléogène, est honorable. A l'aube des temps, de gigantesques roches primitives se trouvaient là où la Forêt Noire et les Vosges, ses voisines, se font face, l'une sur la rive droite, l'autre sur la rive gauche du Rhin, telles deux soeurs se ressemblant comme deux gouttes d'eau. C'est dans cette «zone de tiraillement de l'écorce terrestre», que s'est constitué un «fossé d'effondrement», si bien que le Rhin dut bifurquer aux environs de Bâle et se creuser un chemin en direction de la Mer du Nord. C'est la raison pour laquelle ces deux massifs montagneux, sillonnés de vallées interminables et bordés de villes hors pair telles que Fribourg, Strasbourg et Bâle, tombent abruptement vers la plaine basse que forme le cours supérieur du Rhin. C'est, dans le Triangle constitué par les trois pays au sud-ouest de l'Allemagne, une constellation de trois splendides astres d'où émergent les tours élancées de cathédrales gothiques qui n'ont pas leurs pareilles. Cette région, en passe de sceller une union fraternelle au niveau européen est plaque tournante et barrière à la fois. Au sud, la Forêt-Noire confine avec la Suisse, à l'est avec les contreforts du Jura souabe, autrement dit avec le Lac de Constance et est limitrophe de la France, à l'Ouest. La ligne européenne de partage des eaux suit le tracé de la ligne de faîte de ses collines. A certains endroits, les eaux de source coulent même parallèlement, les unes descendant, il est vrai, vers le Rhin, les autres en direction du Danube. Le Rhin et le Danube faillirent d'ailleurs se serrer la main dans la célèbre Gorge de la Wutach, près de Neustadt/Bonndorf, mais le Rhin, jeune gaillard au tempérament fougueux finit par «couper l'herbe sous le pied» du Danube qui, à cet endroit, n'est encore qu'un mince filet d'eau, de sorte que la Wutach renonça, en ces temps fort reculés, à faire un grand détour pour rejoindre la Mer Noire et préféra se jeter en catimini dans les bras du Rhin, en son cours supérieur.

Il y aurait encore beaucoup de choses à dire sur les tours de passe-passe et l'humeur capricieuse de la nature. Mais l'«histoire de l'Homme» est, elle aussi, complexe et déroutante. Nous ne la ferons pas commencer à l'âge de la pierre, mais à l'époque où vivaient les Celtes, qui, du point de vue historique sont les premiers à être «saisissables». Des découvertes spectaculaires faites à une époque récente montrent que les Celtes possédaient déjà un niveau de civilisation fort développé et que celle-ci s'étendait bien au-delà de cette région du nord des Alpes. Avant le début de l'ère chrétienne, ils entrèrent pourtant en conflit avec les Romains pour avoir marché sur les brisées de ces derniers, furent battus et, au cours du troisième siècle, finalement envahis par les Alamans .Ces Alamans, qui se nommaient eux-mêmes «Sueben» (Souabes), refoulèrent à leur tour les Romains, s'affirmant en vainqueurs jusqu'à nos jours. «Allemands» c'est ainsi que les Français dénomment, aujourd'hui encore, leurs voisins, ce qui, il est vrai, ne change en rien au fait que des «Alamans» se retrouvent aussi bien en Alsace qu'à la pointe nord-ouest de la Suisse.

Ce qu'ils ont laissé à la postérité est, avant tout, le dialecte alemanique que Johann Peter Hebel a si bien su manier que même le prince parmi les poètes, Goethe, ne put se retenir d'en faire l'éloge.

Depuis longtemps déjà, les distinctions phylogéniques ont perdu de leur importance et de leur influence. Politiquement parlant, la Forêt-Noire a appartenu pendant une certaine période à la Bade, un grand-duché de droit napoléonien, qui regroupait sous un même toit, libéral, les Palatins, au nord jusqu'à Mannheim, les Franconiens et les Alamans avant de contracter mariage avec le Bade-Wurtemberg, à l'issue de la deuxième guerre mondiale. Ainsi, la ville de Stuttgart accéda-t-elle au rang de capitale de l'Etat du sud-ouest, tandis que l'orpheline que Karlsruhe était devenue par là, dut se contenter d'être la «Résidence du Droit». La logique voudrait qu'un chapitre relatif aux antécédents dynastiques de cette région soit intercalé à cet endroit, mais cela reviendrait à retracer l'histoire d'une mosaique de «tapis rafistolés» dont était constitué l'empire allemand de l'époque. Nous ne mentionnerons que les plus remarquables des protagonistes de son histoire: les Zähringen qui, jusqu'au XIIe siècle, ont laissé de leur passage les témoignages les plus importants. Les pays du sud de l'Allemagne firent ensuite partie de «l'Autriche antérieure». Mais c'est la Maison de Bade qui, finalement, rassembla sous son aile l'ensemble du pays. Nous retrouverons les traces de ces dynasties en faisant la visite de quelques-unes des villes de cette région. Mais la Forêt-Noire demeure, une fois pour toutes, le royaume des arbres.

Der Schliffkopf, von dem aus die Aufnahme gemacht wurde, gehört zu den markantesten Punkten des Nordschwarzwaldes. Hier gabelt sich der Weg hinab ins Rheintal oder nach Osten via Freudenstadt. Bis hinauf auf den Bergrücken ziehen sich endlose Wälder und Hochmoore, die im Sommer zu langen Wanderungen und im Winter bei Schnee zum Langlauf einladen.

The Schliffkopf, from which this picture was taken, is one of the most prominent features of the northern Black Forest. Here the path forks down into the Rhine Valley or eastwards via Freudenstadt. Endless woods and upland moors stretch up onto the ridge, a tempting prospect for long walks in summer or cross-country skiing in winter.

Le Schliffkopf, d'où a été prise cette photographie, fait partie des aspects les plus saisissants du nord de la Forêt-Noire. C'est là que bifurque la route menant, d'un côté, vers la vallée du Rhin, et de l'autre vers l'est, via Freudenstadt. D'interminables forêts et des tourbières de montagne s'étendent sur sa ligne de faîte, invitant, en été, à des randonnées pédestres, en hiver et par temps de neige, au ski de fond.

Die Wutach-Schlucht, in die man bei Bonndorf und Rötenbach von unterschiedlichen Stellen aus „einsteigen" kann, ist das größte und eindrucksvollste Naturschutzgebiet. Das Wasser der Wutach, das sich ganz tief in die geologisch bemerkenswert reichhaltigen Formationen hineingegraben hat, verschwindet gelegentlich völlig im Waldesdunkel, um dann wieder über ein paar Felsen hinabzuspringen. Die Wutach-Schlucht, ein Eldorado für Wanderer, ist dreißig Kilometer lang und von der Außenwelt beinahe völlig abgeschnitten.

Wutach Gorge, accessed from various places in the neighbourhood of Bonndorf and Rötenbach, is the largest and most impressive of nature conservation areas. Occasionally the waters of the Wutach, cutting deeply into the remarkably rich geological formations, disappear completely into the darkness of the forest, only to emerge again, leaping down across a group of rocks. Wutach Gorge, a paradise for walkers, is 30 km (19 miles) long and almost totally cut off from the outside world.

La gorge de la Wutach à laquelle il est possible d'accéder en différents endroits, près de Bonndorf et de Rötenbach, est la plus vaste et la plus remarquable des réserves naturelles existantes. L'eau de la Wutach qui s'est infiltrée dans les profondeurs des formations géologiques et de leurs multiples couches sédimentaires, disparaît parfois complètement dans l'obscurité pour rejaillir un peu plus loin et dévaler la pente en retombant sur les rochers. La gorge de la Wutach, eldorado des randonneurs, a trente kilomètres de long et est presque entièrement coupée du monde extérieur.

Das Freilicht-Museum „Vogtsbauernhof" in Gutach bei Hausach lockt zu allen Jahreszeiten Tausende von Besuchern an. Auf dem weiten Areal sind die Bauformen des Schwarzwaldhofes mustergültig repräsentiert. Die Stirnseite des Hofes ist meist auch die mit Blumen reich geschmückte Schauseite.

The "Vogtsbauernhof" open-air museum in Gutach, near Hausach, attracts thousands of visitors all year round. In the extensive museum grounds you can see examples of different types of Black Forest farmhouse buildings. The front of the farmhouse, the "show side", is usually richly decorated with flowers.

Quelle que soit la saison, le Musée de plein air «Vogtsbauernhof», à Gutach, près de Hausach, attire des milliers de visiteurs. Les formes architecturales qu'épouse la ferme de la Forêt-Noire sont représentées de façon exemplaire sur le vaste terrain de ce domaine. Le front de la ferme, abondamment fleuri, est en même temps son «beau côté».

Zünftige Bergwanderer werden im Schwarzwald oft mit einem alles überragenden Aussichtsturm belohnt, so auch am Brandenkopf. Wer vom Kinzigtal ins verträumt gelegene Mühlbachtal abzweigt, hat diesen Gipfel ständig vor Augen. Von oben sieht man dann rundum auf die Rebhügel der Ortenauer Vorgebirgslandschaft.

In the Black Forest, expert mountain walkers are often rewarded with vantage points affording outstanding views, like this one here on the Brandenkopf. Anyone branching off from the Kinzig Valley along the sleepy Mühlbach Valley will have this mountain constantly in sight. From the top you can enjoy an all-round view across the vine-covered slopes of the Ortenau foothills.

Les randonneurs aguerris partant à l'assaut des sommets de la Forêt-Noire, sont souvent dédommagés de leurs efforts en découvrant une tour d'où se dégage un beau point de vue sur la région environnante. Ainsi en est-il du Brandenkopf. Celui qui aura quitté la vallée de la Kinzig pour s'engager dans celle, idyllique, du Mühlbach, ne perd jamais de vue ce sommet. Des hauteurs, le regard embrasse les vignobles tapissant, de tous côtés, les collines des contreforts de l'Ortenau.

Das Wasserschloß Inz-
lingen gehört zu den Klein-
oden, die besondere Auf-
merksamkeit verdienen. Es
liegt in der Nähe von Lörrach nahe dem Rheinknie
bei Basel. Das 1563 er-
richtete Schlößchen ist vor-
züglich erhalten und wird
von einem Heiligen Ne-
pomuk aus dem 18. Jahr-
hundert bewacht.

Inzlingen moated castle is
one of those gems which
deserve special attention. It
is not far from Lörrach,
near the sharp bend in the
Rhine at Basle. Built in
1563, the castle has been
wonderfully well preserved
and is watched over by an
18th-century effigy of St
Nepomuk.

Entouré de douves, le
château d'Inzlingen
compte parmi les joyaux de
cette région qui méritent
une attention particulière.
On le trouvera dans les
environs de Lörrach, non
loin du «Genou» que des-
sine le Rhin près de Bâle.
Ce petit château, érigé en
1563, est en excellent état
de conservation et gardé
par un Saint-Nepomuk
datant du XVIIIe siècle.

Man muß schon Glück haben und einen sonnigen Herbst- oder Wintertag erwischen, dann bietet sich vom Belchen aus ein unvergleichlicher Blick auf die gesamte Alpenkette, mit den Berner Alpen als „Höhepunkt". Bei besonders guter Fernsicht kann man gelegentlich sogar den 400 km entfernt gelegenen Mont Blanc mit bloßem Auge entdecken.

If you are lucky enough to be there on a sunny autumn or winter day, from the Belchen you have an incomparable view right along the Alpine mountain chain, culminating in the Bernese Alps. On a particularly clear day even Mont Blanc, 400 km (250 miles) away, is visible to the naked eye.

Si la chance lui sourit, le visiteur pourra, par une journée d'automne ou d'hiver bien ensoleillée, jouir d'une vue incomparable sur la chaîne des Alpes et en voir même le »point culminant«, les Alpes bernoises. Lorsque la vue est particulièrement bien dégagée, il apercevra peut-être aussi, à l'œil nu, le Mont Blanc, à 400 km de distance.

Was wäre Paris ohne den Eiffelturm, New York ohne die Freiheitsstatue, der Schwarzwald ohne das *Schwarzwaldhaus*? Das ist ein gewagter Vergleich, aber dennoch berechtigt. Denn wie jede „Stadtlandschaft" von ihren markanten Bauten geprägt wird, so der Schwarzwald von dem Hof, der seinen Namen trägt. Man wird auf der ganzen weiten Welt kaum einen Landstrich finden, dessen Gesicht, ja dessen Seele so sehr von der Form und Gestalt seiner Häuser bestimmt worden ist. Schon deshalb sollte man nie vergessen, daß es sich auch beim Schwarzwald um eine von Menschenhand gestaltete „Kulturlandschaft" handelt. Allerdings mit einem entscheidenden Unterschied zu urbanen Siedlungen. Die unvergleichliche Harmonie des Schwarzwaldhauses rührt daher, daß es vom Scheitel bis zur Sohle naturwüchsig entstanden ist. Der Boden gab alles her, wessen es zu seiner Errichtung bedurfte: den rostbraunen Gneis für die Mauern; die mit der Axt behauenen Baumstämme für die gewaltigen Fachwerke; das Stroh und später die handgeschnitzten Schindeln, die zu Tausenden an Dach und Hauswänden befestigt werden mußten. Das Gebälk mancher Höfe ist dreihundert Jahre alt, ohne faul und morsch zu werden, weil es der Windzug konserviert hat.

Solche Höfe konnten höchst herrschaftlich sein, von besitzstolzen Bauernfürsten bewohnt. Niemals standen sie in Reih und Glied, sondern immer einsam und raumverdrängend, von einem Kranz an Nebengebäuden umgeben: Die eigene Kapelle mit Altar und Gebetsstühlen gehörte dazu; der Backofen, in den die großen Brotlaibe gesteckt wurden; die Mühle, in der man die Bretter schnitt oder sogar die autonome Stromversorgung sicherte; das „Libding" (Leibgedinge), in das die Alten zogen, wenn der Hoferbe die Braut heimbrachte und „Kindersegen" erwarten durfte.

Jeder Hof hatte seine individuelle Lage. Meist setzte man ihn auf die Fallinie des Berghanges, der Sonne zugewandt, auf den Lauf der Wege und Wasser achtend, gegen Sturm und Blitzschlag von mächtigen Laubbäumen gesichert. Behütet beinahe bis auf den Boden hinab von einem riesigen Walmdach, das Mensch und Tier unter seiner Haube beherbergte. Noch ist diese Herrlichkeit nicht völlig versunken, noch findet der Wanderer diese alten Höfe, deren Urtyp das Heidenhaus ist. Sein Stammbaum reicht bis zum Dreißigjährigen Krieg zurück. Viele Anwesen sind inzwischen fachkundig und mit denkmalpflegerischer Sorgfalt, aber dennoch funktionsgerecht für moderne landwirtschaftliche Betriebe restauriert worden. Trotzdem gibt es keinen Zweifel: Der Schwarzwaldhof kämpft um sein Überleben. Sein ehrwürdiges Alter hat ihn inzwischen auch museumsreif werden lassen. Einige Prachtexemplare kann man auf dem „Vogtsbauernhof" in Gutach (bei Hausach im Kinzigtal) bewundern. Dort lassen sich auch die Stilentwicklung und das reiche „Innenleben" der bäuerlichen Wohngemeinschaften studieren. Es beginnt in der Küche, wo hoch unterm Dach im kalten Rauch die Speckseiten geräuchert wurden. Es setzt sich fort in der guten Stube mit ihren „Herrgottswinkeln" und führt bis zur Ofenbank, der sogenannten „Kunscht", in deren wärmster Ecke der „Bur" seinen „Winterschlaf" gehalten hat, während Bäuerin und Mädge Wolle spinnen mußten.

Nehmen wir Abschied von der musealen Welt. Denn im Schwarzwald sind die Traditionen immer noch lebendig. Es gibt Täler, in denen die alten Frauen ihre Trachten nicht nur sonntags, sondern auch werktags zur Arbeit tragen, dann jedoch aus bescheidenem blauen Tuch. Aber welch einen hinreißenden Anblick bieten sie, wenn sie ihr festtägliches „Häs" aus dem Schrank holen und mit ihrem „Kopfschmuck" zur Kirche pilgern. Das Elztaler Schäppele mit seinen aufgetürmten Glasperlen, der rote Bollenhut aus Gutach, die buntbestickten Samtmieder, sie verwandeln jede Frau in eine Schönheit, gleichgültig, ob jung oder alt.

Doch wenn schon von Traditionen die Rede ist, soll nicht vergessen werden, daß auch der Schwarzwälder wenigstens einmal im Jahr „Narrenfreiheit" braucht. Da tobt er sich aus, kurz aber heftig, versteckt sich hinter schaurigen Masken oder undurchsichtigen Larven, setzt an zum „Narrensprung" von Rottweil, macht gewaltigen Lärm mit Pritschen und Saublodere (Schweinsblasen), hängt sich große Schellen um den Hals oder verwandelt sich in einen feuerroten „Schuddig" mit schwarzer Holzmaske. Am „schmutzige Dunschtig", dem „schmutzigen Donnerstag", spielen sie allerorten verrückt und beschwören nach unverkennbar heidnischem Brauch sämtliche Dämonen und Hexen. Die schwäbisch-alemannischen Narrenzünfte in den Hochburgen zu Haslach, Hausach, Elzach, Rottweil halten das Brauchtum am Leben. Erst am „Aschermittwoch" geht es wieder christlich zu, dann streuen sich die Narren Asche aufs Haupt und beginnen zerknirscht die Fastenzeit.

What would Paris be without the Eiffel Tower, New York without the Statue of Liberty, the Black Forest without the Black Forest house? This is a bold comparison, but a justified one. For just as every townscape is characterised by its prominent buildings, the Black Forest is symbolised by the house which bears its name. Scarcely anywhere else in the whole wide world will you find an area whose appearance, whose very soul is so much determined by the shape and style of its houses. For this if for no other reason one should never forget that with the Black Forest we are talking about a man-made landscape. Admittedly, in a very different way from urban settlements. The incomparable harmony of a Black Forest house rests in the fact that it is a product of Nature from top to toe. Everything needed for its construction came from the earth: the rust-coloured gneiss for the walls; the tree trunks felled with axes for the massive half-timber beams; the thatch and later the hand-carved shingle tiles that had to be fastened in their thousands to roof and external walls. The timberwork of many of these houses is 300 years old, and has not decayed or rotted because the winds have preserved it.

Such homes, inhabited by wealthy farmers proud of their possessions, could be utterly magnificent. They were never built in rows or joined to others, but always detached and spaciously arranged, surrounded by a ring of outbuildings, including a private chapel with altar and pews; a bread oven in which the enormous loaves were baked; the mill, where planks were sawn or which even provided an independent power supply; and the "Libding" or annex which the older generation moved to when the heir to the farm brought home his bride and might expect to be blessed with offspring.

Each house had its own individually chosen position. Usually it was built on a steep mountain slope, facing the sun, paying attention to watercourses and tracks, secured against storms and lightning by massive deciduous trees. It was protected by a gigantic sloping roof reaching almost down to the ground, sheltering both man and beast beneath its canopy. This magnificence has not entirely disappeared. The hiker will still come across these old farmsteads, the prototype of which is the moorland house. Its pedigree dates back to the Thirty Years' War. Meantime many estates have been restored with expert care and due attention to conservation, but also functionally, to the standards required of modern agricultural businesses. Nevertheless there is no doubt that the Black Forest house is struggling for survival.

Meantime its venerable age has also made it suitable museum material. A few splendid examples can be admired at the "Vogtsbauernhof" farm museum in Gutach near Hausach in the Kinzig Valley, where you can also study the development of architectural style and the rich "inner life" of the farmstead. This starts in the kitchen where sides of bacon are cold-smoked high up under the roof. It continues in the sitting room with its "crucifix corner" and ends up by the hearth, the so-called "Kunscht," in the cosiest corner of which the farmer took his "winter nap" while his wife and the farm girls had to spin wool.

Let's bid farewell to the world of museums. For in the Black Forest traditions are still alive. There are valleys where the old women wear their traditional costumes not just on Sundays but on weekdays too, though the weekday version is made only of simple blue cloth. But what an enchanting sight they make when they take their best "Häs" or traditional dresses out of the cupboard and wend their way to church wearing their headdresses. The Elztal "Schäppele" headdress with its piled up glass beads, the red "Bollen" hat from Gutach and the colourfully embroidered velvet bodices transform every woman into a beauty, no matter whether young or old.

But while we're talking of tradition we should not forget that even the Black Forester needs to be able to "go mad" once a year. Then he lets off a short but energetic burst of steam, hides behind horrendous masks or heavy make-up, does the Rottweil "fool's leap" (Narrensprung), makes a tremendous racket with fool's wands and pig's bladders, hangs large bells around his neck or transforms himself into a fiery red "Schuddig" with a black wooden mask. On "Schmutziger Dunschtig," or "Dirty Thursday" they all pretend to be mad and call up all the demons and witches—an unmistakably heathen tradition. The Swabian-Alemannic fools' guilds in the strongholds of Haslach, Hausach, Elzach, and Rottweil keep old customs alive. Not until Ash Wednesday does Christianity take hold again. Then the remorse-stricken fools strew ashes on their heads and begin the period of Lent.

Que serait Paris sans la Tour Eiffel, New York sans la statue de la Liberté, la Forêt-Noire sans la «maison de la Forêt-Noire»? Cette comparaison est certes hardie, mais ne manque pas de bien-fondé. En effet, tout comme le «paysage urbain» porte le sceau de ses édifices les plus marquants, la Forêt-Noire se définit, elle, par la ferme qui porte son nom. On aura peine à trouver dans notre vaste monde une contrée dont la physionomie, voire l'âme, soient, à ce point, empreintes par la forme et le style de ses maisons. Cela suffit à nous rappeler que la Forêt-Noire est une terre de civilisation façonnée par l'homme. Une différence profonde la distingue toutefois des agglomérations urbaines. L'harmonie incomparable qui se dégage de la «maison de la Forêt-Noire» vient de ce qu'elle est, de «pied en cape», un produit de la nature environnante. Le sol a tout fourni des éléments nécessaires à son édification: le gneiss de couleur rouille pour ses murs; les troncs d'arbres dégrossis à la hâche pour ses énormes pans de bois; le chaume et, plus tard, les bardeaux sculptés à la main. La charpente de certaines fermes a trois cents ans et n'est ni pourrie ni vermoulue, le vent coulis ayant contribué à la préserver. Les fermes de ce genre pouvaient adopter le caractère de véritables demeures seigneuriales. Elles n'étaient, d'ailleurs, jamais disposées selon un ordre rigoureux, mais occupaient toujours une position isolée dans la nature, au milieu de vastes espaces de terres et étaient sceintes d'une couronne de bâtiments annexes: la chapelle, propriété du paysan, avec l'autel et les prie-dieu; le four où l'on cuisait les grosses miches de pain; le moulin où l'on coupait les planches et qui pourvoyait aussi la ferme en électricité; le «libding», bâtiment où emménageaient les vieux lorsque l'héritier amenait à la ferme sa fiancée.

Chacune de ces fermes occupait une position bien à elle. Le plus souvent, elle était construite sur la ligne de chute du versant, tournée vers le soleil, respectait le tracé des chemins et des cours d'eau et était protégée de la tempête ainsi que de la foudre par les majestueuses couronnes de ces arbres. Son énorme toit en croupe qui touchait presque le sol, abritait hommes et bêtes et les enveloppait comme d'une houppelande. Cette magnificence n'a pas encore totalement disparue et le promeneur pourra rencontrer sur son chemin ces vieilles fermes construites sur le modèle archaïque de la maison propre au paysage de landes du nord de l'Allemagne. Son arbre généalogique remonte jusqu'à la Guerre de Trente Ans. Entretemps, un grand nombre de ces fermes ont été restaurées avec le soin et la compétence normalement apportés à la protection des sites et

monuments historiques, tout en demeurant adaptées aux exigences d'une exploitation agricole moderne. Toutefois, il ne fait aucun doute que la ferme de la Forêt-Noire lutte pour sa survie.

Dans l'intervalle, son âge respectacle en a fait une pièce de musée. Quelques spécimens, parmi les plus beaux, peuvent être admirés à la ferme «Vogtbauernhof», à Gutach (près de Hausach, dans la vallée de la Kinzing).

Faisons nos adieux à cet univers de musée. En Forêt-Noire, les traditions sont, en effet, demeurées bien vivantes Il est des vallées où les vieilles femmes portent leurs costumes traditionnels non seulement le dimanche mais en semaine, costumes qui, pour le travail quotidien, sont faits d'un tissu bleu, plus modeste. Mais quel ravissement pour l'oeil lorsqu'elles sortent de leurs armoires leur «Häs», tenue de fête agrémentée d'une coiffe, et se rendent ensuite à l'église. Le «Schäppele» que l'on rencontre dans la vallée de l'Elz, fait d'un amoncellement de perles de verre, le «Bollenhut», chapeau traditionnel à pompons rouges de Gutach, les corselets de velours, garnis de broderies multicolores font une reine de beauté de toute femme, qu'elle soit jeune ou vieille.

Puisqu'il est question ici de traditions, nous n'oublierons pas de souligner que l'habitant de la Forêt-Noire a lui aussi besoin, ne serait-ce qu'une fois l'an, de la «liberté du fou». C'est alors qu'il donne libre cours à son allégresse, se dissimulant derrière des masques terrifiants ou des loups impénétrables et qu'il prend son élan pour aller faire le «Saut du Fou» à Rottweil, tout cela dans un fracas de battes et de «Saublodere» (de vessies de cochon), s'affublant de gros grelots, accrochés à son cou et se métamorphosant en «Schuddig», au déguisement d'un rouge flamboyant et au masque de bois noir. C'est le «schmutziger Dunschtig», le «jeudi sale» donc, que, dans tous les villages, les habitants se déchaînent pour de bon, conjurant sorcières et démons, suivant une coutume indubitablement paienne. Les «Confréries de Fous» souabes-alemaniques qui se sont constituées dans les fiefs du carnaval tels que Haslach, Hausach, Elzach et Rottweil maintiennent vivante la coutume. Ce n'est que le Mercredi des Cendres que les «fous» font pénitence et que, bien à contre-cœur, ils commencent le carême.

Das aus zahllosen Kunstperlen handgefertigte „Schäppele" ist der älteste und schönste Kopfschmuck für die jungen Mädchen und Frauen im Schwarzwald. Der in Gutach (Ortenaukreis) beheimatete Bollenhut wurde erst später „erfunden", hat aber inzwischen alle Konkurrenten im Bekanntheitsgrad übertroffen. Am ehesten entdeckt man die alten Trachten bei den sommerlichen Trachtenumzügen.

The "Schäppele", handmade with a multitude of pearl beads, is the oldest and most attractive of Black Forest headdresses for girls and women. The "Bollenhut", which has its home in Gutach in the Ortenau district, is a later invention that has surpassed its rivals in terms of widespread recognition. You are most likely to come across traditional costumes in summertime costume parades.

Le «Schäppele», coiffe faite à la main et constituée d'innombrables perles synthétiques est la plus ancienne et la plus belle des parures dont les jeunes filles et les femmes de la Forêt-Noire ornent leurs têtes. Le «Bollenhut», qui se porte à Gutach (dans la circonscription d'Ortenau) ne fut «inventé» que plus tard, mais a, entretemps, supplanté tous ses concurrents pour ce qui est de la célébrité. C'est en été, à l'occasion des défilés en costumes régionaux, qu'on aura le plus de chance de faire la découverte de ces tenues traditionnelles.

Das Föhrental ist eines jener zahllosen versteckten Seitentäler, die von den Haupttälern abzweigen und meist in einer „Sackgasse" enden. Es liegt am Eingang zum Glottertal. Im Föhrental finden sich besonders schöne alte Höfe. Dieser hat mindestens 200 Jahre auf dem Buckel.

The Föhren Valley is one of those many hidden side valleys which branch off from a main valley and usually lead into a "dead end". It lies at the entrance to the Glotter Valley. The Föhren Valley has some particularly beautiful old farmsteads. This one is a good 200 years old.

La Föhrental est l'une des innombrables vallées transversales qui partent des vallées principales et bifurquent dans une autre direction pour finir le plus souvent en cul-de-sac. Le point de départ de cette vallée se situe à l'entrée de la Glottertal. On y trouve d'anciennnes fermes d'une rare beauté. Celle que l'on voit représentée ici a au moins deux cents ans.

Wie die alten Bauernstuben aussahen, läßt sich nirgendwo besser studieren als im „Vogtsbauernhof". Besonders anheimelnd ist das Leibgedinghäusle, in dem die „Alten" nach der Übergabe des Hofes an die nächste Generation eine Wohnung fanden. In der kleinen Stube ist alles aus Holz, bis auf den alten Kachelofen. Der Herrgottswinkel und die Schwarzwalduhr machen den Raum wohnlich.

The "Vogtsbauernhof" is the best place to study what farm living quarters looked like in the old days. The "dower house" is particularly snug. It is where the "old people" went to live after handing over the farm to the next generation. In the little living room everything apart from the tiled stove is made of wood. The prayer corner and the Black Forest clock add a homely touch.

Nulle part ailleurs qu'au «Vogtsbauernhof», une ferme-musée, on ne saurait mieux étudier l'habitat tel qu'il se présentait dans la salle où se réunissaient le paysan et sa famille. Une atmosphère de douce intimité se dégage de la petite maison, dite «Leibgedinge», où les «Vieux» emménageaient après avoir cédé la ferme à la génération suivante. Dans la petite salle, tout, à l'exception du poêle de faience, est en bois. Le «coin du Seigneur» et le coucou confèrent à la pièce une chaude atmosphère.

Der Rottweiler Narrensprung ist jedes Jahr einer der Höhepunkte der alemannischen Fasnet. Unter den Augen vieler Besucher ziehen die Narrenzünfte durch die Hauptstraße dieser wunderbaren alten Reichsstadt. Die Springnarren bedienen sich eines großen Reisigbesens, die Schellenträger vertreiben mit ihrem „Gschell" den Winter.

Each year the Rottweil "Narrensprung" or "Fool's Leap" is one of the highlights of Alemannic Fasnet. Watched by numerous visitors, the fools' guilds parade along the main street of this wonderful ancient Imperial city. The leaping fools wield big birch-brooms, whilst the bell-wearers jingle their bells to drive out winter.

Chaque année, le «Narrensprung» (Le Saut des Fous) de Rottweil est l'un des points culminants du Fasnet, le carnaval alémanique. Sous les yeux de nombreux visiteurs, les «Confréries de Fous» défilent à travers la rue principale de cette ancienne et magnifique ville d'empire. Bondissant, les «Fous» se servent d'un grand balai de bouleau et les porteurs de grelots agitent leurs sonnettes pour tenter de chasser l'hiver.

Wo schon die Römer baden gingen: die berühmten Badeorte

Ja die alten Römer, was haben wir ihnen nicht alles zu danken: Den Wein, das Recht, den ganzen Reichtum ihrer mediterranen Kultur und vor allem natürlich — ihre luxuriösen Bäder. Zwar kamen sie am Beginn der Neuzeit nicht gerade in friedlicher Absicht, aber jedenfalls haben sie die in dunklen Wäldern (nigrae silvae) hausenden Germanenstämme aus dem Dämmerschlaf der Geschichte geweckt und ihnen soviel Zivilisation beigebracht, daß wir noch heute davon zehren. Bestes Beispiel: die zahlreichen Bäder, die sich am Westrand des Schwarzwaldes in schönster Lage eingenistet haben. Schon ihre Namen sind Programm, heißen sie doch Baden-Baden und Badenweiler. Jedenfalls hatten die rauhen Legionäre, die sich ständig für militärische Höchstleistungen fit halten mußten, einen untrüglichen Spürsinn für heiße Quellen. Die Kunst, sie mit unterirdischen Warmluftkanälen komfortabel auszubauen, beherrschten sie ohnehin.

Ein warmes oder kaltes Bad, von heilkräftigen Wassern gespeist — das war zu allen Zeiten der Inbegriff von Wohlbehagen, eine köstliche Verheißung von Gesundheit und Verjüngung. Kein Wunder, daß die Baden-Badener Balneologen ihr neuestes Luxusbad mit dem kaiserlichen Titel Caracalla-Therme versehen haben und täglich Tausende in die Stadt an der Oos locken. Die römische Erbschaft ist damit aber nicht aufgezehrt. Diese Badeorte waren nämlich immer auch Traumplätze für herrschaftliche Wohnsitze in milder Luft und vornehmer Lage am Saum von Wäldern und Weinbergen.

Wem die Krone unter den Badeorten gebührt, darüber kann man gar nicht streiten, denn das hängt von den Wehwehchen, von den Leiden oder Leidenschaften ab, deretwegen man sie aufsucht. Es ist aber eine alte Weisheit, daß man schneller gesund wird, je besser es um die Unterhaltung bestellt ist. In diesem Punkt ist Baden-Baden bis heute an Glanz und Berühmtheit von niemandem übertroffen worden. Ende des vorigen Jahrhunderts galt dieses „Weltbad" als „Vorstadt" von Paris. Man sah in seinen Mauern jede Menge gekrönter Häupter. Im Spielkasino — der heißen Quelle des schnellen Reichtums — ist sogar der russische Dichter Dostojewskij aufgetaucht. Er ließ den Rubel rollen und schilderte dann in seinem aufwühlenden Roman „Der Spieler" alle Freu-

den und Leiden eines unheilbaren Hasardeurs. Auf der Lichtenthaler Allee mit ihrem herrlichen Baumbestand promenierten die feinen Leute, die in erlesenen Spitzenhotels eine ganze Suite belegten. Dieser Glanz der belle epoque mag zwar etwas Patina angesetzt haben, doch der Gast ist noch immer Majestät. Und wenn im Frühjahr in der Rheinebene die Iffezheimer Rennen „laufen", dann kann man noch immer die mondänen Damen mit ihren wagenradgroßen Hüten ebenso bewundern wie die edlen Vierbeiner.

Damit kann Badenweiler am Südzipfel des Schwarzwaldes nicht konkurrieren. Seine Lage jedoch auf halber Höhe am Fuß des Blauen ist durchaus ebenbürtig. Badenweiler residiert wie auf einem Herrensitz über das ganze Markgräflerland, dessen Anmut alles übertrifft. Hier haben die Römer ihre größte Baderuine nördlich der Alpen hinterlassen, das längst erloschene Geschlecht der Zähringer hat eine Burg errichtet, und die Winzer bauen in ihren Rebbergen einen feinen Tropfen an, der sich im Charakter von allen anderen Gewächsen des badischen Weinbaugebietes unterscheidet. Während bei Baden-Baden, das einige der renommiertesten Weindörfer gleich eingemeindet hat, ein gehaltvoller „Mauerwein" gekeltert und in Bocksbeuteln abgefüllt wird, ist der Markgräfler „Gutedel" von der sanfteren Art, nicht so wuchtig wie der „Kaiserstühler", aber bekömmlich zu allen Tageszeiten. Vorausgesetzt, man hält sich an die Empfehlung der Einheimischen: Süepfle muesch, nit sufe! Im hochdeutschen Klartext heißt das: Du mußt ihn langsam schlürfen, aber nicht saufen.

Wer die Landkarte des Schwarzwaldes studiert, wird aber neben den beiden Spitzenreitern noch eine Menge attraktiver, gesundheitsfördernder „Bäder" entdecken: Bellingen ist ein „heißer" Tip in Richtung Basel. Bad Krozingen bei Freiburg beherbergt die großen Rehabilitationszentren. Im nördlichen Landesteil findet sich ein ganzer Kranz von Bädern: Peterstal; Herrenalb, am Ende des Albtals nahe bei Karlsruhe; auf der schwäbischen Rückseite im „Gäu" unweit von Stuttgart liegen in verborgener Schönheit Teinach, Wildbad, Liebenzell, Rippoldsau und schließlich das bekannte Solbad Dürrheim vor den Toren von Donaueschingen.

In allen diesen Bädern kursiert ein bisher noch nicht widerlegtes Gerücht, nach dem es Kurgäste geben soll, von denen die Heilkraft des Weines noch höher veranschlagt wird als die der Thermen. Beweisen läßt sich nichts. Aber wahrscheinlich liegt die Wahrheit in der Mitte: In Maßen und mit Verstand genossen, hat die Natur nichts Besseres zu bieten.

Where once the Romans bathed: The famous spas

Think of all the things we have to thank the ancient Romans for: wine, the law, the whole richness of their Mediterranean culture and above all of course—their luxurious baths. Admittedly at the beginning of modern times they did not come with exactly peaceful intentions, but in any case they aroused the Germanic tribes, who at that time were still dwelling in dark forests, from their historic slumber and taught them so much about civilisation that we are still enjoying the fruits of it today. The best example of this are the numerous spas nestling in the most lovely of spots along the western fringe of the Black Forest. The very names of Badenweiler and Baden-Baden are enough to spell out their programme. Anyway, the rough legionaries, who had to keep themselves fit for military exertions, had an infallible nose for hot springs. And of course they were well versed in the art of making the best of them by equipping them with subterranean warm-air ducting.

A hot or cold bath, nurtured by healing waters, has always been the quintessence of well-being, an exquisite promise of health and rejuvenation. No wonder that the Baden-Baden balneologists have given their latest luxury bath the royal-sounding name of Caracalla Thermal Spring, tempting thousands of people every day to the town on the River Oos. But that is not the end of the Roman legacy. For these spa towns have likewise always been ideal sites for grand residences amidst the mild air and genteel locations on the edge of forests and vineyards.

There is no point in arguing about which town is queen of the spas, for that depends on the aches and pains, the suffering or the enthusiasm which has led one to seek them out. However, there is a wise old saying that the better the entertainment the quicker one feels better. In this respect up till now Baden-Baden remains unsurpassed in terms of fame and splendour. At the end of the last century this "world spa" was dubbed a "suburb" of Paris. Any number of crowned heads were to be seen within its walls. Even the Russian poet Dostoevsky turned up at the gaming casino, a favourite spot for getting rich quick. He staked his roubles and then in his turbulent novel "The Gambler" described all the joys and sorrows of an incurable player with fortune. The gentry reserved whole suites in select first-class hotels and promenaded under the magnificent trees along Lichtenthaler Allee. This belle époque grandeur may have acquired the patina of age, but the guest is still king. And in spring when the Iffezheimer horse races take place on the Rhine plain, one can still admire the chic ladies with their cartwheel hats and the noble quadrupeds.

Badenweiler in the southern corner of the Black Forest cannot compete with that. However, it enjoys an equally desirable location in the hills at the foot of the Blue Mountain. Like a ruler's residence, Badenweiler presides over the whole Markgräfler area, unrivalled for its charm. Here the Romans left behind the ruins of the biggest baths north of the Alps. Here too the long extinct Zähringer dynasty built a fortress. In the hillside vineyards the vintners grow a fine class of vine, different in character from all the other grapes of the Baden winegrowing area. In the district of Baden-Baden, which also contains one of the most renowned wine villages, a rich "Mauerwein" is pressed and bottled in the squat round "Bocksbeutel" bottles. The Markgräfler "Gutedel" wine is of a softer type. It is not as heavy as the "Kaiserstühler" and goes down well at any time of day. Provided, that is, that one sticks to the advice of the natives: "Süupfle muesch, nit sufe," in other words, "Sip it slowly, don't swill it down."

Anyone studying a map of the Black Forest will discover, in addition to the two leading contenders, a host of other attractive health "spas." Bellingen is a "hot" tip on the way to Basle. Bad Krozingen near Freiburg is home to the biggest convalescent centres. In the northern part of the area there is a whole garland of spas, notably Peterstal and Herrenalb at the end of the Alb Valley not far from Karlsruhe. In the "Gäu" area not far from Stuttgart on the other side of Swabia you will find the hidden beauty of Teinach, Wildbad, Liebenzell, Rippoldsau and finally the salt-water spa of Dürrheim just outside Donaueschingen.

An as yet uncontradicted rumour circulates in all these spas, which says that there are some spa visitors who value the healing powers of wine higher than those of the thermal baths. It can't be proved one way or the other. Presumably the truth lies somewhere in between. Taken in moderation and with common sense, Nature offers nothing better.

Ah, nos ancêtres les Romains, que ne leur devons-nous pas: le vin, le droit, toute la richesse de leur civilisation méditerranéenne et, avant tout, bien sûr, leurs luxueux établissements de bains. Ce n'est certes pas dans la meilleure intention qu'ils nous arrivèrent, au début des temps modernes, mais ils ont au moins le mérite d'abord secoué de leur engourdissement les tribus germaines vivant , à l'époque, dans de sombres forêts (nigrea silvae) et de leur avoir fait don d'une culture telle que nous en tirons encore profit de nos jours. Le meilleur exemple en sont les nombreuses villes d'eaux, venues se nicher dans les plus beaux sites, en bordure ouest de la Forêt-Noire. Leurs noms sont on ne peut plus évocateurs: Baden-Baden, Badenweiler. En tout cas, les légionnaires plutôt rustres possédaient un sens inné des sources thermales. Ils maîtrisaient, par ailleurs, l'art de les doter de confort grâce à l'aménagement de canaux souterrains où circulait l'air chaud.

Un bain alimenté par des eaux aux vertus curatives, qu'il soit chaud ou froid, a, de tous temps, été l'essence même du bien-être, une délicieuse promesse de santé et de jouvence. Nul ne s'étonnera donc que les balnéologues de Baden-Baden aient conféré au plus récent de leur établissement de bains publics le titre, impérial, de «Thermes de Caracalla» et que celles-ci attirent chaque jour, dans cette ville des bords de l'Oos, des milliers de personnes.

Inutile de se disputer quant à la question de savoir à laquelle des stations thermales revient la palme; cela dépend, en effet, des petits bobos, du genre d'affection de la personne s'y rendant ou tout simplement de la passion qui l'anime. Mais il est un adage très ancien qui veut que plus les possibilités de divertissement sont nombreuses, plus la guérison progresse vite. Sur ce point, Baden-Baden est demeuré inégalée et aucune ville n'a été en mesure, jusqu'à nos jours, de lui disputer la palme pour ce qui est de l'éclat et de la célébrité. Vers la fin du siècle passé, cette «ville d'eaux internationale» passait pour être une «banlieue de Paris». Elle vit défiler une foule de têtes couronnées et le casino − «source chaude» de toute fortune vite faite − apparaître, un jour, le poète russe Dostoieski. Il y brassa du rouble et décrivit, par la suite, dans son bouleversant roman, «Le Joueur», toutes les joies et les souffrances des passionnés atteints du mal incurable qu'est l'amour du jeu. Les gens distingués, qui louaient une suite dans de somptueux hôtels , flânaient dans la «Lichtenthaler Allee», bordée de magnifiques arbres. Une certaine patine a beau avoir recouvert ces splendeurs de la Belle Epoque, l'hôte y est demeuré roi. Et, lorsque les courses hippiques ont lieu, au printemps, à Ifferzheim, dans la plaine du Rhin, on peut encore admirer aussi bien les dames du monde, coiffées de leurs chapeaux à larges bords, que les nobles quadrupèdes.

Badenweiler, située à la pointe sud de la Forêt-Noire, ne saurait faire face à cette concurrence. Son site, à mi-hauteur du «Bleu», lui permet, un tant soit peu, de relever le défi. Comme du haut d'une demeure seigneuriale, Badenweiler domine tout le pays du Margräferland, dont le charme est incomparable. C'est là que les Romains laissèrent à la postérité les plus vastes thermes du nord des Alpes, thermes aujourd'hui en ruines, là aussi que les Zähringen érigèrent un château fort et que les vignerons cultivent un vin fin se distinguant, par son caractère, de tous les autres cépages de la région viticole badoise. Alors que, aux alentours de Baden-Baden − qui a incorporé à sa commune quelques-unes des localités viticoles des plus renommées −, on produit un vin de muraille corsé, logé dans le «Bocksbeutel», une bouteille aux flancs plats, le «Gutedel» issu du Markgräflerland, est d'une saveur plus douce et moins robuste que le vin du Kaiserstuhl, mais il est fort digeste et peut se boire à toutes les heures de la journée. A condition, il est vrai, de s'en tenir aux recommandations des gens du pays: «süepfle muesch, nit sufe», ce qui, en haut allemand, revient à dire›tu dois le savourer à petits coups et non t'en abreuver.»

Celui qui se penche avec attention sur la carte de la Forêt-Noire, découvrira, en dehors de ces deux vedettes que sont Baden-Baden et Badenweiler, une foule de villes d'eaux attrayantes, aux effets bénéfiques pour la santé: Bellingen, en direction de Bâle, est à recommander. Bad Krozingen, près de Fribourg, abrite les grands centres de réhabilitation. La partie nord du pays est parsemée de ville d'eaux: Peterstal, Herrenalb, au fin fond de la vallée de l'Alb, non loin de Karlsruhe. Du côté souabe, dans le «Gäu», à peu de distance de Stuttgart, se trouvent Teinach, Wildbad, Liebenzell, Rippoldsau, toutes de vraies beautés cachées, et enfin, la ville d'eaux salines qu'est Dürrheim, aux portes de Donaueschingen.

Dans toutes ces villes d'eaux circule une rumeur tenace, selon laquelle certains curistes feraient passer la vertu curative du vin avant celle des eaux thermales. Le prouver est impossible. Mais la vérité est probablement entre les deux: bu modérément et raisonnablement, c'est le plus beau cadeau que la nature a su nous faire.

Baden-Baden schmiegt sich lieblich in das sanft geschwungene Oostal. Von allen Seiten kann man einen wunderbaren Blick auf diese „vornehme" Stadt gewinnen, die alles bietet: Schlösser, Kirchen, Badeeinrichtungen mit Komfort, einen Spielsaal und eine Promenade, auf der man viele elegante Menschen bewundern kann.

Baden-Baden nestles charmingly in the gently rolling countryside of the Oos Valley. From all sides you have a wonderful view of an elegant town which has everything: palaces, churches, baths boasting every comfort, a gaming casino and a promenade where you can admire fashionable society.

Baden-Baden se blottit délicieusement dans la vallée légèrement ondulante de l'Oos. Quel que soit l'angle sous lequel il la contemple, cette ville «distinguée» offre au regard du spectateur sa splendeur et ses attraits: ses châteaux, ses églises, ses bains dotés de tout le confort imaginable, un casino et une Promenade où il pourra admirer des gens tout aussi distingués.

Klein und vornehm ist Wildbad, das ebenso wie Liebenzell und Teinach nur eine knappe Autostunde von Stuttgart entfernt liegt. Besonders beliebt ist die Bergbahn, die auf die Hochebene des Sommerbergs hinauftuckert. Wer sich wie im Morgenland fühlen möchte, besuche die prunkvollen Ruheräume des Graf-Eberhard-Bades, das im maurischen Stil angelegt wurde.

Wildbad, which like Liebenzell and Teinach is only an hour by car from Stuttgart, is small and select. The mountain railway, which chugs its way up onto the Sommerberg plateau, is especially popular. Anyone wanting to cool off in Oriental fashion should visit the splendid restrooms of the Graf Eberhard baths, designed in the Moorish style.

Wildbad qui, tout comme Liebenzell et Teinach n'est qu'à une heure de route environ de Stuttgart, est une élégante petite station climatique. Le chemin de fer de montagne qui grimpe en soufflant jusque sur le haut-plateau du Sommerberg est particulièrement prisé. A celui qui voudra se retrouver au pays du Levant, nous recommandons une visite des salles de repos des bains Graf Eberhard, aménagées dans le style mauresque.

Bad Liebenzell mit seinen
radiumhaltigen Thermal-
quellen ist eines der meist-
besuchten Heilbäder im
nördlichen Schwarzwald.
Es liegt im Talkessel am
unteren Nagoldtal, wird
überragt von einer gewaltigen Burgruine und ist um-
geben von bewaldeten Ber-
gen. Nach den „Strapazen"
der Bade- und Trinkkuren
findet man im Kurpark
Ruhe und Schatten.

Bad Liebenzell with its
thermal springs containing
radium is one of the most
frequented watering places
in the northern Black
Forest. It lies in a hollow in
the lower part of the
Nagold Valley, towered
over by an immense ruined
castle and surrounded by
wooded mountains. Here
in the Kurpark you can
find peace and shade after
the "exertions" of bathing
in and drinking the healing
waters.

Bad Liebenzell est l'une
des villes d'eaux les plus
fréquentées du nord de la
Forêt-Noire en raison de
ses sources thermales à
teneur de radium. Domi-
née par les ruines d'un
château médiéval aux
imposantes dimensions et
entourée de collines boi-
sées, la ville se blottit dans
la vallée encaissée du cours
inférieur de la Nagold.
Après les «supplices» des
cures d'eau minérale et de
balnéothérapie, la tranquil-
lité et l'ombre attendent le
curiste dans le Parc de
cette station climatique.

Der liebe Gott hat zwischen dem südlichen und dem nördlichen Schwarzwald eine klare Trennlinie gezogen. Sie führt von Offenburg, das man auch als Bauchnabel des Schwarzwaldes bezeichnen könnte, das Kinzigtal hinauf bis Hausach, wo sich die Wege in Richtung Freudenstadt oder Villingen-Schwenningen gabeln. Das nördliche Tor zum Schwarzwald ist Pforzheim, das zugleich den Brückenkopf zwischen dem badischen und dem schwäbischen Landesteil bildet. Zum Südschwarzwald gibt es im landschaftlichen Charakter, in der geologischen Formation, in der Bewaldung und in der Besiedlungsgeschichte beträchtliche Unterschiede. Im Norden herrscht der rote Buntsandstein vor. Das führt zu kantigeren Felsformationen. Die Täler sind schärfer eingekerbt, und die Wälder, meist Tanne und Fichte, haben sich nahezu nirgendwo von den Hängen vertreiben lassen. Dieser Waldreichtum hat auch seine Schatten. Denn es gibt kaum kahlgeschorene „Grinden", die sich über die Baumgrenze hinaus erheben. Nur wenige Berge übersteigen die Tausendmetergrenze. Der höchste, weithin beherrschende Gipfel ist die 1150 Meter hohe Hornisgrinde.

Hier muß ein kurzes (ganz persönliches) Kapitel zum sogenannten Waldsterben eingeblendet werden. Jedem sei empfohlen: Macht die Augen auf, und ihr werdet sehen: Die Waldschäden sind nicht so massiv, wie vielfach behauptet wird. Gewiß kann nicht geleugnet werden, daß er da oder dort — wie etwa am „Katzenkopf" am Kniebis — Krankheitssymptome aufweist, die Grund zur Besorgnis geben. Solche Gefahren dürfen nicht verharmlost, sie sollten aber auch nicht übertrieben werden, wie es vielfach geschieht. Eines ist aber trotz aller Meinungsunterschiede unstrittig: Der Wald bedarf unserer Fürsorge. Er ist ökologisch der beste Klimaschutz.

Ungeachtet der Schadstellen besitzt aber gerade auch der nördliche Schwarzwald einen eigenen, unverwechselbaren Zauber. Auf seinem Rücken zieht sich, von Baden-Baden bis nach Freudenstadt, die Schwarzwaldhochstraße hin, die nicht nur ein Tummelplatz für Autofahrer ist, sondern auch eine Zufahrt für unzählige Wandertouren. Die „Hornisgrinde" ist über den hochromantischen Mummelsee oder über andere Rastplätze im einstündigen Fußmarsch leicht zu erreichen. Von dort oben sieht man im Osten nichts als uferlose Wälder und im Westen — wenn die dampfende Rheinebene die Sicht nicht stört — die brüderlichen Vogesen. Die schönsten, himmelhohen Bäume, um doch auch ihr Loblied zu singen, stehen in den Teuchelwäldern bei Freudenstadt, der Hauptstadt des schwäbischen Schwarzwaldes. Nur Baiersbronn auf der anderen Kammseite kann da noch mithalten. Ebenso lohnenswert ist das Hochmoorgebiet unweit vom Schliffkopf mit dem Wildsee und Hornsee als ewig nassen Badewannen aus der Eiszeit.

Wer von den Bergen heruntergewandert und dann im mittelbadischen Ländle landet, dem geht das Herz auf über dem Reichtum dieser Vorgebirgslandschaft, in der Milch und Honig zu fließen scheinen. So saftig und fleischig wie in der Gegend von Bühl sind die Zwetschgen nirgendwo. Der mittelbadische Obstgarten bietet alles, was die Sonne gedeihen läßt. Und der Wein, der in der Ortenau bei Offenburg wächst, ist so gut, daß Elisabeth II. aus England bei ihrem ersten Besuch im Badischen ein zweites Gläschen vom „Roten" erbeten haben soll. Das ist ebensowenig eine Erfindung wie der deftige Abenteuerroman des „Simplicius Simplicissimus", den der „Schultheiß" Hans Jakob Christoffel von Grimmelshausen aus Renchen im 17. Jahrhundert sehr zur Freude aller Literaturkenner geschrieben hat. In diesem mittelbadischen Paradiesgärtlein kann man in vielen anheimelnden Dorfkneipen „bechern" und „spachteln", trinken und essen, wie nur noch im Umland von Freiburg.

Damit sind die Reize dieser Landschaft aber noch lange nicht erschöpft. Wer von Rastatt aus — wo der „Türkenlouis", der berühmte Retter vor den Heerscharen aus dem Land des Halbmondes ein großartiges Schloß gebaut und ganz im tiefsten Wald seiner Gattin Amalia den köstlichen Witwensitz „Favorite" hinterlassen hat — das Murgtal hinauffährt, kommt durch eine tiefe Furche, die hier durch den Nordschwarzwald führt. Überall finden sich feingeputzte Ortschaften, die zum Verweilen einladen. Es ist gar nicht so lange her, da fuhren die „Flözer" in abenteuerlicher Fahrt mit ihren gewaltigen Baumstämmen über Murg, Nagold und Enz in den Rhein hinab, Kopf und Kragen für ein paar Gulden aus der Hand der holzarmen Holländer riskierend. Die „Murgschifferschaft", um ihren ehrbaren Zunftnamen zu nennen, läßt ahnen, wie hart man früher im Schwarzwald sein Geld erarbeiten mußte. Während er doch heute eher dazu da ist, daß man es dort springen läßt.

God has drawn a clear line of separation between the southern and northern Black Forest. It runs from Offenburg, which one might describe as the Black Forest's navel, up the Kinzig valley to Hausach, where the paths fork towards Freudenstadt or Villingen-Schwenningen. The northern gate to the Black Forest is Pforzheim, which also forms the bridgehead between the Baden and Swabian parts of the region. In terms of the type of scenery, geological formation, afforestation and the history of settlement here there are considerable differences from the southern Black Forest. In the North, new red sandstone predominates. That leads to more angular rock formations. The valleys are more deeply cut and the mountain slopes almost entirely covered by fir and pine trees. However this abundance of forest also has its downside. For there are scarcely any "shaven heads" rising above the treeline. Only a few of the mountains rise above the 1,000-metre (3,281-foot) boundary. The highest mountain, dominating the landscape for miles around, is the 1,150-metre (3,773-foot) Hornisgrinde.

Here we must insert a short (very personal) chapter about the so-called dying of the forest. Everyone should be recommended to open their eyes, then they would realise that the forest demage is not as serious as it often claimed. Certainly one cannot deny that here and there—as for example on the Kniebis "Katzenkopf"—it is showing symptoms of disease which give cause for concern. Such risks should not be brushed aside, but neither should they be exaggerated, as is often the case. Despite all differences of opinion, one fact remains undisputed: the forest needs our care and attention. Ecologically it is the best protection for our climate.

Regardless of the areas of damage, the northern Black Forest possesses its very own unmistakable magic. The Black Forest highway from Baden-Baden to Freudenstadt runs across its back. This highway is not only a hotbed of motorists, but also an approach road for innumerable hiking tours. The Hornisgrinde can easily be climbed in an hour taking the wonderfully romantic Mummelsee route or via other picnic spots. From its summit, towards the East you see nothing but boundless forests, and to the West—if the mists over the Rhine valley plain don't obscure the view—the fraternal Vosges. But the loveliest, tallest trees, to sing their praise, are in the Teuchel woods near Freudenstadt, the capital of the Swabian Black Forest. Only Baiersbronn on the other side of the ridge can match it. A visit to the high moorland region not far from the Schliffkopf mountain with the Wildsee and Hornsee reminding one of two Ice Age "baths" is equally worthwhile.

Descending from the mountains to the countryside of central Baden, your heart will miss a beat at the richness of these foothills, where milk and honey seem to flow. Nowhere are the little "Zwetschgen" plums as juicy and succulent as in the Bühl area. The central Baden orchards produce everything that flourishes in the sunshine. And the vines that grow in the Ortenau near Offenburg are so good that on her first visit to Baden Queen Elizabeth II is said to have asked for a second glass of the "red." This story is no more fictional than "Simplicius Simplicissimus," the ribald novel written in the 17th century by Mayor Hans Jakob Christoffel von Grimmelshausen, much to the delight of all connoisseurs of literature. In this little central Baden Garden of Paradise you can eat and drink in many homely village pubs as nowhere else except in the area around Freiburg.

But that by no means exhausts the delights of this region. There is the magnificent castle in Rastatt, built by "Turkish Louis," rescuer of the army legions from the land of the crescent moon, and the exquisite "Favorite" widow's residence, hidden deep in the forests, which he left to his spouse Amelia. Travelling from here up the Murg valley, you come across a deep furrow cutting into the northern Black Forest. Everywhere you will find well-kept villages inviting you to tarry awhile. It is not so long ago that raftsmen used to take mighty tree trunks on the hazardous journey along the Murg, Nagold and Enz rivers down to the Rhine, risking life and limb for a few guilders from the wood-hungry Dutch. The "Murg Society of Boatmen" to give it its proper guild title, gives an idea of how tough it used to be to earn a living in the Black Forest—whereas nowadays its purpose in life seems to be to give people the opportunity to spend what they have earned.

Le Bon Dieu a tracé une ligne de démarcation très nette entre le nord et le sud de la Forêt-Noire. Elle part de Offenburg — que l'on pourrait également appeler le nombril de la Forêt-Noire —, longe la Vallée de la Kinzig et mène jusqu'à Hausbach, sur les hauteurs, pour bifurquer finalement dans deux directions, menant l'une vers Freudenstadt, l'autre vers Villingen-Schwenningen. Pforzheim marque, au nord, l'entrée de la Forêt-Noire et constitue, en même temps, une tête de pont entre la partie badoise et souabe du pays. Comparée au sud de la Forêt-Noire, cette région en est profondément différente pour ce qui est du caractère de son paysage, de sa formation géologique, de son boisement et de l'histoire de son peuplement. Le grès rouge bigarré domine au nord, et a engendré la forme anguleuse de la roche qui la caractérise. Les vallées y sont plus encaissées et les forêts composées, pour la plupart, de sapins et d'épicéas qui, presque partout, se sont aggripés opiniâtrement aux versants. Seuls quelques sommets dépassent les mille mètres, et le plus élevé parmi eux est le Hornisgrinde qui, de ses 1150 mètres d'altitude, domine le paysage environnant.

Qu'il nous soit permis d'intercaler, à cet endroit, un chapitre bref (et très personnel), relatif à ce que l'on appelle généralement la mort de la forêt. Un conseil à tous nos lecteurs: ouvrez les yeux et vous verrez: les dégâts causés à la forêt ne sont pas aussi considérables qu'on le prétend d'ordinaire. Certes on ne peut nier que, ici et là, comme par exemple au «Katzenkopf», sur le massif du Kniebis, elle ne manifeste quelques signes de maladie susceptibles de faire naître une certaine inquiétude. De tels dangers ne sauraient être minimisés, mais il ne faudrait pas non plus en exagérer l'importance, comme il en est souvent le cas. Malgré ces divergences de vues, une chose demeure indiscutable: la forêt a besoin de notre protection. En matière d'écologie et de climat, elle représente le plus efficace bouclier qui soit. Si l'on fait abstraction de ses lésions, la Forêt-Noire — notamment sa partie nord — possède une magie enchanteresse qui n'appartient qu'à elle. Sur sa crête, de Baden-Baden à Freudenstadt, serpente la «Schwarzwaldhochstraße» (la Route des Crêtes) qui est une voie d'accès à d'innombrables itinéraires de randonnées pédestres. Le promeneur atteindra aisément la «Hornisgrinde» en une heure de marche en passant par le très romantique lac de Mummelsee ou par d'autres étapes. Du sommet, on découvre, à l'est, une infinité de forêts et, à l'ouest, les jours où les brumes montant normalement du Rhin n'obstruent pas la vue — les Vosges, ses soeurs. Les plus beaux de ses arbres cyclopéens se trouvent dans les «Teuchelwälder», à proximité de

Freundenstadt, capitale de la Forêt-Noire souabe. Seul Baiersbronn, de l'autre côté de la ligne des crêtes, peut soutenir la comparaison. La région de tourbières de montagnes qui s'étend non loin du Schliffkopf et comprend les lacs de Wildsee et de Hornsee, cuvettes éternellemnt humides datant de la période glaciaire, est également digne d'une visite.

Le randonneur qui descend de la montagne et pose le pied au coeur du Pays de Bade, ne peut que se sentir comblé de bonheur à la vue de l'opulence de ces contreforts montagneux où semblent ruisseler le lait et le miel. Nulle part ailleurs, les quetsches ne sont aussi juteuses et charnues que dans la région de Bühl. Le jardin qu'est la Bade moyenne offre tout ce que le soleil fait pousser. Et le vin, cultivé dans la contrée de Ortenau, près de Offenburg, est si bon que, lors de sa première visite au Pays de Bade, Elisabeth II, reine d'Angelterre, aurait demandé à ce qu'on lui verse un second petit verre du «rouge». Cette anecdote tient aussi peu de la fable que le roman d'aventures fort polisson, «Simplicius Simplicissimus», que Hans Jakob Christoffel von Grimmelshausen, maire du village de Renchen, écrivit, au XVIIe siècle, à la grande joie de tous les connaisseurs en matière de littérature. Presque toutes les petites auberges aux senteurs de terroir que compte ce paradis de la Bade moyenne, invitent à «caresser la bouteille» et à «faire bonne chère».

Les charmes de cette région ne sont pas épuisés, tant s'en faut. Celui qui remonte la vallée de la Murg, venant de Rastatt — où «Türkenlouis», le fameux margrave qui sauva son pays en repoussant les armées du pays du Croissant de Lune, fit construire un splendide château, ainsi qu'une délicieuse résidence, «Favorite», au plus profond de la forêt à l'intention de son épouse Amalia, qui y passa son veuvage —, s'enfonce dans un sillon profond creusé à travers la Forêt-Noire. Partout on peut admirer de petites bourgades coquettes qui invitent à s'y attarder. Il n'y a pas très longtemps encore, les flotteurs de bois, montés sur d'énormes troncs d'arbres, dévalaient, intrépides, les rivières que sont la Murg, le Nagold et l'Enz afin de rejoindre le Rhin, risquant leur vie pour quelques maigres florins que leur payaient les Hollandais à qui le bois faisait défaut. La «Compagnie de Navigation sur la Murg», tel était, en effet, le nom vénérable de cette corporation, nous permet de nous imaginer au prix de quels efforts l'argent se gagnait, jadis, en Forêt-Noire. Alors qu'aujourd'hui, cette dernière serait plutôt là pour nous le faire débourser.

Forbach ist der Hauptort
des mittleren Murgtales,
das den nördlichen
Schwarzwald bis hinauf
nach Baiersbronn zer-
furcht. Etwas oberhalb der
Ortschaft wird die Murg
von einer feingliedrigen,
mit Schindeln überdachten
Holzbrücke überspannt.
Noch weiter hinauf ist die
Murg für das Murg-
Schwarzenbach-Werk zur
Elektrizitätsversorgung auf-
gestaut.

Forbach is the main town
in the central Murg Valley,
which cuts through the
northern Black Forest right
up to Baiersbronn. Some
way above the town a fine-
ly proportioned covered
wooden bridge crosses the
Murg. Still further
upstream the Murg is
dammed to provide elec-
tricity for the Murg-
Schwarzenbach works.

Forbach est le chef-lieu de
la vallée moyenne de la
Murg qui sillonne la partie
nord de la Forêt-Noire et
s'étire jusque sur les hauteurs, à Baiersbronn. En
amont, à quelque distance
de cette localité, la Murg
est enjambée par un pont
de bois finement travaillé
et couvert d'un toit de bardeaux. Plus haut, l'eau de
la Murg a été retenue pour
y aménager l'usine de
Murg-Schwarzenbach qui
approvisionne la région en
électricité.

Am Kamm des Nord-
schwarzwaldes entlang
führt Deutschlands älteste
Ferienstraße direkt zum ro-
mantischen Mummelsee.
Er liegt tausend Meter
hoch am Fuß der Hornis-
grinde, ist rund wie eine
Scheibe und läßt sich in
einer halben Stunde leicht
umrunden. Früher sollen
sich hier Nixen getummelt
haben, heute sind es Heerscharen von Touristen. Nur
im tiefsten Winter hat man
den See für sich allein.

Germany's oldest holiday
route runs along the ridge
of the northern Black
Forest directly to the
wonderfully romantic
Mummelsee. The lake is
situated 1,000 metres above
sea level at the foot of the
Hornisgrinde. It is circular
like a plate, and you can
easily walk round it in half
an hour. Water-nymphs are
said to have frolicked here
in bygone days, but
nowadays all you will find
are tourist hordes. Only in
the depths of winter can
you have the lake all to
yourself.

Longeant la crête des montagnes de la Forêt-Noire
dans sa partie nord, la plus
ancienne route touristique
d'Allemagne mène directe-
ment au très romantique
Mummelsee. Il s'étend au
pied de la Hornisgrinde, à
1000 mètres d'altitude, et a
la rondeur d'un disque
dont le pourtour peut être
parcouru en une demi-
heure. Les nymphes qui, si
l'on en croit la légende,
s'ébattaient jadis en ces
lieux, ont fait place à des
légions de touristes. Ce
n'est qu'au cœur de l'hiver
que l'on se retrouve seul à
seul avec le lac.

Der Marktplatz von Freudenstadt war und ist das gelungene Beispiel einer eindrucksvollen Stadtarchitektur aus der Renaissancezeit. Im Krieg völlig zerstört, gilt der nach dem Schema des Mühlespiels angelegte Platz auch als Musterbeispiel eines vorbildlichen Wiederaufbaus, der Altes und Neues harmonisch miteinander zu versöhnen versteht.

The market square in Freudenstadt has always been an impressive example of Renaissance town architecture. Completely destroyed in the war, the square, which is laid out in chequerboard pattern, is also a model of exemplary restoration, achieving a harmonious blend of old and new.

La Place du Marché de Freudenstadt, de style Renaissance, est et demeurera un modèle d'architecture urbaine réussie. Intégralement détruite pendant la guerre, cette place dont la disposition est inspirée du jeu de la marelle, est également considérée comme étant un modèle de reconstruction ayant su harmonieusement réconcilier l'ancien et le moderne.

Altensteig im oberen
Nagoldtal, das mit seinen
guterhaltenen Giebel-
dächern am steilen Berg-
hang liegt, bietet ein male-
risches Bild. Nach alter
Bautradition befinden sich
Schloß und Kirche noch
höher als die Bürgerhäuser.
Das Domizil der Grafen
von Hohenberg ist im
schwäbischen Fachwerkstil
erbaut worden.

Altensteig in the upper
Nagold Valley, with its
well-preserved gable roofs
ascending the steep moun-
tainside, presents a pic-
turesque scene. In keeping
with time-honoured
building tradition, the
castle and the church are
even higher up than the
townspeople's houses. The
residence of the Counts of
Hohenberg is constructed
in Swabian half-timbered
style.

Altensteig, que l'on découvre en remontant la vallée
de la Nagold et dont les
toits à pignons s'aggrippent
au versant escarpé de la
colline, revêt un aspect des
plus pittoresques. Selon
une tradition architecto-
nique séculaire, le château
et l'église surplombent les
maisons bourgeoises. La
demeure du comte de
Hohenberg a été réalisée
dans le style souabe des
maisons à colombage.

Am Schwarzwaldrand gibt
es zahlreiche Burgen.
Ortenberg imponiert durch
seine beherrschende Lage
an der Eingangspforte zum
Kinzigtal. Von der alten
Festung aus staufischer
Zeit sind zwar nur wenige
Spuren geblieben, um so
stolzer präsentiert sich die
neoromantische Burg, die
von den Weinbergen der
Ortenau umgeben ist.

There are a large number
of castles along the
perimeter of the Black
Forest. Ortenberg enjoys
an impressively command-
ing position at the entrance
to the Kinzig Valley.
Though only a few traces
remain of the old Staufen
fortress, these merely
reinforce the grandeur of
the neo-Romantic castle,
surrounded by the Ortenau
vineyards.

De nombreux châteaux
médiévaux bordent la Forêt
Noire. Ortenberg impres-
sionne par la position
dominante qu'il occupe, à
l'entrée de la vallée de la
Kinzig. S'il n'est resté que
de rares vestiges de
l'ancienne forteresse
remontant à l'époque des
Hohenstaufen, le château
de style néo-romantique se
dresse, lui, avec d'autant
plus de majesté, surplom-
bant les vignobles de
l'Ortenau qui le ceintu-
rent.

Darf ich ausnahmsweise eine kleine Geschichte aus meiner Jugend erzählen? Selbstverständlich keinen losen Schwank, sondern eine wahre Begebenheit. Deshalb ist sie auch völlig harmlos, jedoch voller köstlicher Erinnerungen. — Mein „Vater selig", wie man früher im Badischen gesagt hat, Jahrgang 1878 und ein armer „Wälderbub" aus dem wundervollen Simonswälder Tal unweit von Freiburg hat es mit seinem hellen Kopf bis zum studierten Finanzrichter in der einstigen Landeshauptstadt Karlsruhe gebracht, er blieb aber seiner sieben Kinder wegen zeitlebens ein besserer Hungerleider, dem der Geldbeutel keinerlei „Sprünge" erlaubte. So boten sich bei der Entscheidung über die Sommerferien nur zwei Möglichkeiten: entweder in heimatlichen Gefilden bei bäuerlichen Verwandten im „Spicher", wo man Brombeeren und Heidelbeeren sammeln, den Stall ausmisten oder mit den Kühen auf die Weide „fahren" durfte. Oder ein Aufenthalt bei der gestrengen Großmutter in Stockach am Bodensee, die kein Staubkorn auf ihrem Parkettboden duldete, dafür aber wunderbar kochen konnte. In der Nähe des Überlinger Sees gelegen, war Stockach vor allem deshalb begehrt, weil man dorthin nur mit der Schwarzwaldbahn gelangen konnte, die hinter Offenburg langsam den Berg hinaufkeuchte, pausenlos in nachtschwarze Tunnel fuhr, dann plötzlich das Licht erreichte, um gleich wieder in den nächsten Tunnel einzutauchen. Man sah es mit eigenen Augen oder fühlte es in der Nase kitzeln, wie sie den Roßschweif ihrer schwarzen Rauchfahne stolz im Winde wehen ließ, wie sie sich um die eigene Achse drehte, so daß man die Spur der Geleise eine Bergstufe tiefer vor sich liegen sah und wie sie in Sommerau schließlich den stolzen Scheitelpunkt ihrer Klettertour erreichte. Doch merkwürdig: Auf der anderen Seite ging es nur gemächlich wieder hinunter bis nach Donaueschingen, wo angeblich die Donau entspringt, während sie in Wahrheit von Brigach und Breg zuweg gebracht wird, die von weither der Residenz der Fürsten von Fürsten-

berg zufließen. Eine halbe Fahrtstunde hinter Donaueschingen, wo die hochgelegene „Baar" ein Scharnier zwischen Schwarzwald und Bodensee bildet, sah man die Vulkankegel des Hegau, und von da war es dann nur noch ein Katzensprung bis Stockach, wo uns die Großmutter mit der Weisung empfing: Die Schuhe werden sofort ausgezogen, hier sind die Filzlatschen!

Seit über hundert Jahren hat die Schwarzwaldbahn nichts von ihrer Faszination verloren, auch wenn sie längst keine halbe Tagesreise mehr kostet. Noch heute gilt sie als technische Meisterleistung, die dem Bauingenieur und Naturfreund Robert Gerwig ein Denkmal in Triberg beschert hat. Er fand in den achtziger Jahren des vergangenen Jahrhunderts nicht nur den kürzesten, sondern auch den kostengünstigsten Weg. Statt aufwendige Brücken zu bauen, bohrte er sich in den Berg hinein, ließ die Bahn bei Triberg drei große Schleifen ziehen und überwand auf einer „Luftlinie" von nur elf Kilometern 448 Meter Höhenunterschied.

Für die Wirtschaft im mittleren Schwarzwald begann damit so etwas wie ein Höhenflug, denn Triberg entwickelte sich alsbald zum Touristenzentrum, und die Produktion der weltbekannten Schwarzwalduhren, die ursprünglich auf den einsamen Höhen zwischen Schönwald und Waldau gefertigt wurden, bekam durch die Verbesserung der Verkehrswege entscheidende Impulse zur industriellen Fertigung. Wunderbar bemalte alte, noch immer funktionierende „Zeitmesser" kann man im Triberger Heimatmuseum besichtigen. Doch die reichste Sammlung findet man einige Kilometer weiter entfernt im „Deutschen Uhrenmuseum" zu Furtwangen, wo die Paradestücke bäuerlicher Tüftelarbeit aus mehreren Jahrhunderten zu sehen sind. Wer schließlich zu Fuß auf den Spuren der Vergangenheit wandeln will, macht sich von Triberg aus auf den „Uhrenweg", der über Stock und Stein rings um den mittleren Schwarzwald führt.

Zurück aber noch einmal zur Eisenbahn. Nicht minder attraktiv ist die „Höllentalbahn", die von Freiburg über Titisee-Neustadt wiederum nach Konstanz führt und einige Stationen mit so aufregend schönen Namen berührt wie Himmelreich, Höllsteig und Hirschsprung. Auch sie muß über Brücken und Viadukte eine Differenz von 600 Metern überwinden, ehe sie in gemächlicher Fahrt dem Schwäbischen Meer, sprich Bodensee, zusteuern kann. Weniger „bucklig", dafür aber wirtschaftlich um so bedeutsamer, ist die Bahnlinie am Oberrhein, die Basel mit Konstanz verbindet und einiges für die (kommerzielle) Verbrüderung zwischen Deutschen und Schweizern getan hat.

Might I by way of exception rela a little story from the days of m youth? It's something that real happened, not just a funny story. Thus i something quite innocuous, but full delightful memories. My late father wa born in 1878, a poor "forest boy" from th glorious Simonswald Valley not far fro Freiburg. He was a bright lad and succeede in qualifying as a financial court judge in th former state capital of Karlsruhe. Howeve on account of his seven children, he staye poor all his life, and had no money for e travagances of any kind. Thus whe deciding where to go for our summe holidays, there were only two options. Th first was to return to home pastures and sta with country relatives in the "Spicher where we could pick blackberries and bilbe ries, muck out the cowshed or drive the cov to pasture. The other was to go and stay i Stockach on Lake Constance in the home our strict grandmother, who wouldn tolerate a speck of dust on her parquet floo but was a wonderful cook. The main reaso for preferring Stockach, situated not fa from the Überlinger See, was that the onl way of reaching it was by the Black Fore railway, which past Offenburg slowly coug ed and spluttered its way up the mountai passing without a break through tunnels a black as night, then suddenly emerging int the light of day, only to plunge straight bac into the next tunnel. You could see or sens by the tickling in your nose how it waved i black pillar of smoke in the wind like horse's tail, how it turned back on itself s that you could see the line of the tracks fu ther back down the mountain, and how finally reached the proud vortex of its clim at Sommerau. But remarkably, on the othe side there was only a gradual descent bac down to Donaueschingen, said to be th source of the River Danube, though in fac the honour belongs to the Rivers Brigac and Breg, flowing from far off to the seat the Princes of Fürstenberg. Half an hour o from Donaueschingen, where the "Baar forms a high-altitude link between the Blac Forest and Lake Constance, one could se the volcanic peak of the Hegau and fro there it was only a stone's throw to Stockac There our grandmother greeted us with th instruction to take off our shoes straigl away and put on our felt slippers!

In a hundred years the Black Forest railwa has lost none of its fascination, even thoug the journey has long since ceased to take half a day. Still now it is looked on as a brilliant technical achievement. A monument in Triberg pays tribute to civil engineer and nature-lover Robert Gerwig, who, in the 1880s, discovered not only the shortest, but also the cheapest route. Instead of building costly bridges, he drilled into the mountainside, had the track make three great loops near Triberg, and thus overcame a difference of 448 metres (1,470 feet) in height over a stretch of 11 kilometres (7 miles) "as the crow flies."

With the construction of the railway the central Black Forest economy took off, for Triberg soon developed into a tourist centre, and the improvement in transport connections provided the decisive impetus for the industrial production of the world-famous Black Forest clocks, whose birthplace are the lonely highlands between Schönwald and Waldau. You can admire the wonderfully painted old "timepieces" still working in the Triberg Folk Museum. But the richest collection is situated a few miles further away in the German Clock Museum in Furtwangen, where the best examples of several centuries of intricate rural craftsmanship are on show. Those who wish to track down the past by Shanks's pony will set out from Triberg along the "Clock Path," which leads up hill and down dale through the central Black Forest.

But back to the railway. The "Höllental" railway is no less attractive, running from Freiburg via Titisee-Neustadt again to Constance, passing through stations with wonderfully evocative names like Himmelreich, Höllsteig and Hirschsprung. This too makes use of bridges and viaducts to overcome a height difference of 600 metres (1,969 feet), before wending its leisurely way to the "Swabian Sea," that is, Lake Constance. Less winding, and therefore economically more important, is the Upper Rhine railway connecting Basle with Constance, making its contribution towards fraternal (commercial) relations between Germans and Swiss.

Puis-je exceptionnellement raconter une petite histoire de jeunesse? Non, bien entendu, une quelconque anecdote, mais un fait vécu. C'est une histoire donc bien inoffensive mais en même temps pleine de délicieux souvenirs. «Feu mon père», comme on disait, autrefois, dans le Pays de Bade, vit le jour en 1878. «Gamin des bois», issu d'une famille pauvre de la merveilleuse vallée Simonswald, non loin de Fribourg, et doué d'une grande vivacité d'esprit, il avait fait des études et était devenu juge au Tribunal compétent en matière d'impositions de Karlsruhe, ancienne capitale du land. Mais, ayant eu sept enfants à élever, il demeura, tout au long de sa vie, plus ou moins un «meurt-de-faim» à qui sa bourse ne permettait pas de faire de grands écarts. Ainsi, seules deux possibilités s'offraient à nous lorsque nous devions décider de l'endroit où nous passerions les vacances: soit rester au pays et aller chez des parents agriculteurs au «Spicher», où nous pouvions cueillir des mûres et des myrtilles, nettoyer les écuries ou mener les vaches au pâturage. Soit aller à Stockach, sur les rives du Lac de Constance, chez notre grand-mère qui, de nature sourcilleuse, ne supportait pas le moindre grain de poussière sur son parquet, mais savait si délicieusement cuisiner. Situé à proximité du Lac de Überlingen, Stockach nous était d'autant plus cher que l'on ne pouvait y accéder que par le Chemin de Fer de la Forêt-Noire qui, une fois passé Offenburg, gravissait la montagne en toussotant, traversait en permanence des tunnels d'un noir de suie pour faire sa réapparition dans la lumière du jour et replonger, un instant après, dans la noirceur du tunnel suivant. On pouvait, de ses propres yeux, admirer la fierté avec laquelle il faisait flotter sa crinière de fumée noire dans le vent de la course, ou en ressentir le chatouillis dans les narines, le voir tourner sur son propre axe de sorte qu'on découvrait, devant soi, une terrasse plus bas, le tracé des rails et atteindre finalement le point culminant de son ascension à Sommerau. Chose étrange cependant: de l'autre côté, la descente ne se faisait à petite vitesse que jusqu'à Donaueschingen, là où le Danube prend soi-disant sa source alors qu'en vérité, il ne doit son existence qu'à la Brigach et à la Breg qui, venues de loin, coulent en direction de la Résidence des princes de Fürstenberg. A une demi-heure en voiture de Donaueschingen, là où le haut-plateau de «Baar» forme une charnière entre la Forêt-Noire et le lac de Constance, on apercevait les cônes volcaniques du Hegau et cela signifiait que Stockach n'était plus qu'à deux pas, Stockach où nous attendait grand-mère avec sa sempiternelle consigne: enlever immédiatement vos chaussures et mettez-moi ces pantoufles!

Bien que plus que centenaire, le Chemin de Fer de la Forêt-Noire n'a rien perdu de sa fascination, et cela, même si le trajet ne se fait plus, depuis bien longtemps déjà, en une demi-journée. Il passe encore pour être un chef d'oeuvre de la technique, ce qui valut à Robert Gerwig, l'ingénieur qui le construisit, un fervent de la nature lui aussi, d'avoir sa statue à Triberg. C'est lui qui, vers les années 80 du siècle passé, trouva le chemin à la fois le plus court et le moins onéreux. Au lieu de construire des ponts en grand style, il s'enfonça à travers la montagne et fit décrire aux rails deux larges boucles près de Triberg, triomphant ainsi d'une dénivellation de 448 mètres, alors que la distance à vol d'oiseau n'est que de onze kilomètres.

Ceci permit à la partie médiane de la Forêt-Noire de prendre un essor considérable. Triberg devint très vite un carrefour touristique et la production des coucous, mondialement réputés de la Forêt-Noire, dont les sommets solitaires se dressant entre Schönwald et Waldau furent le berceau, reçut une impulsion notoire grâce à l'amélioration des voies de communication qui permirent leur fabrication industrielle. Ces vieux «compteurs de temps», magnifiquement décorés et fonctionnant encore aujourd'hui, peuvent être admirés au Musée régional de Triberg. Mais la plus riche collection se trouve à quelques kilomètres de là, au Musée allemand de l'Horlogerie (Deutsches Uhrenmuseum) à Furtwangen, où l'on peut voir des pièces rarissimes auxquelles l'ardeur bricoleuse des paysans donna naissance à travers plusieurs siècles. Qui, enfin, désire cheminer sur les traces du passé, empruntera le «Uhrenweg» (le Chemin des pendules) qui mène à travers champs et ceinture la partie médiane de la Forêt-Noire.

Mais revenons une dernière fois au Chemin de Fer. Le «Höllenbahn» (Le train du Val d'Enfer) qui mène de Fribourg, lui aussi, à Constance en passant par Neustadt sur le lac Titisee et traverse des stations aux accents évocateurs telles que «Himmelreich« (Empire céleste), Höllsteig (Montée de l'Enfer) et Hirschsprung (Saut-du-Cerf), exerce un attrait non moindre. Il doit, lui aussi, franchir, au moyen de ponts et de viaducs, une dénivellation de 600 mètres, avant de pouvoir mettre tout doucement le cap sur la Mer souabe qui n'est autre que le lac de Constance. Moins accidentée mais économiquement plus importante est la voie ferroviaire longeant le cours supérieur du Rhin, voie qui relie Bâle à Constance et a contribué, dans une large mesure, à la fraternisation (commerciale) des Allemands et des Suisses.

Deutschlands höchster
Wasserfall befindet sich in
Triberg, das zu den meist
besuchten Fremdenorten
zählt. Wer dort hinaufklet-
tert, wird es nicht bereuen.
Der Weg führt über
Brücken und Stege immer
am Wasser entlang, so daß
nach Bedarf eine kleine
Dusche inbegriffen ist. Triberg liegt besonders ver-
kehrsgünstig an der Ge-
birgsstrecke der Schwarz-
waldbahn und an der
Paßstraße Richtung
Villingen-Schwenningen.

Germany's highest water-
fall is in Triberg, one of the
most popular tourist attrac-
tions. Those who make the
effort to climb up to the
top will not be disap-
pointed. The path leads
across narrow footbridges,
keeping close to the side of
the water, so, if you wish, a
quick shower can be part of
the deal. Triberg enjoys
particularly good transport
connections, being located
on the mountain section of
the Black Forest Railway
and on the road up to the
pass leading to Villingen-
Schwenningen.

Les plus hautes chutes
d'eau d'Allemagne se trouvent à Triberg, qui fait
partie des centres touristi-
ques les plus fréquentés de
la région. Celui qui déci-
dera d'en faire l'escalade
ne le regrettera pas. Le
sentier longe en perma-
nence les chutes d'eau
qu'enjambent ponts et pas-
serelles, de sorte que, si
besoin est, le visiteur aura
droit gratuitement à une
petite douche. Etant située
en bordure de la voie du
Chemin de Fer de la Forêt-
Noire et de la Route du
Col dans la direction
Villingen-Schwenningen,
Triberg bénéficie d'une
position fort avantageuse
sur le plan du trafic.

Die Kuckucksuhr hat viele
Jahrhunderte lang den
Namen des Schwarzwaldes
in alle Welt getragen. Alte
und echte Uhren lassen
sich jedoch kaum noch er-
werben, sondern nur noch
in einigen Museen besichtigen. Heute dominieren die
fabrikmäßig hergestellten
„Blackforest Clocks" den
Markt. Es gibt sie in allen
Größen mit einem maschi-
nell geschnitzten Gehäuse
aus Holz.

For hundreds of years the
cuckoo clock has borne the
name of the Black Forest to
all corners of the earth.
Nowadays genuine old
clocks are virtually unob-
tainable, though you can
see them in several
museums. The market is
dominated by mass-
produced "Black Forest
clocks". You can buy them
in all sizes, with machine-
carved wooden housings.

Depuis des siècles, le coucou a fait la réputation de
la Forêt-Noire à travers le
monde. Les vraies pendules
d'époque sont devenues
presque introuvables et ne
peuvent plus être admirées
que dans quelques musées.
Aujourd'hui, les «Black-
forest clocks», fabriquées
en série, ont envahi le marché. Elles existent dans
toutes les tailles et sont
constituées d'un boîtier de
bois sculpté à la machine.

Größe geht vor Schönheit. Zwar nicht immer, jedoch manchmal. Wer vom Südschwarzwald spricht, muß deshalb beim Feldberg beginnen. Aber nicht nur, weil er mit seinen 1493 Metern alle Rivalen in den Schatten stellt. Er beherrscht auch das ganze Gebirge durch seine zentrale Lage. Dieser Riese mit dem runden Rücken ist nun einmal kein gewöhnlicher Berg, sondern ein „Massiv", das mit Satelliten und Trabanten den gesamten Südschwarzwald in seinen Bann schlägt. Der Feldberg, den die Eiszeitgletscher geduckt haben, ist so wuchtig und vielgestaltig, daß man seinen Anblick nie vergißt. Jeder, der sich ihm von weitem nähert, sucht ihn mit dem Auge und erkennt ihn sofort am Wellenzug seiner vielen Höcker. Auch wenn sich auf seinem Rücken einige garstige Fernmeldeeinrichtungen breitgemacht haben, ist er noch immer ein Magnet, der an manchen Tagen wahre Menschenmassen anlockt, die mit ihren Benzinkarossen aus allen Richtungen, zumeist aber aus dem „Höllental", auftauchen.

Wer schützt die Natur vor den Menschen, wer sorgt dafür, daß sich die Zweibeiner an die vorgezeichneten Trampelpfade halten? Neuerdings sind es fachkundige „Rangers", die in den geschützten Reservaten nach dem Rechten sehen. Bei dieser Idee haben die „grünen Sheriffs" aus den USA Pate gestanden. So gut es geht, sorgen sie dafür, daß nicht alle Blumen ausgerupft und nicht sämtliche Wiesen in Nistplätze für „Wegelagerer" verwandelt werden. Notfalls stellen sie schon einmal einen Strafzettel aus, lassen es aber meist bei einer freundlichen Belehrung bewenden. Diese Aktivitäten nennt man im Bürokratendeutsch „Besucherlenkung" oder „sanften Tourismus".

Von ein paar Rummelplätzen abgesehen, ist und bleibt der Schwarzwald ein Wanderparadies. Insgesamt gibt es 22 000 Kilometer Wanderwege, von der Raute markiert und auf Karten ausgewiesen. Wer gut zu Fuß ist, kann — mit oder ohne Rucksack — in elf Tagen die 270 Kilometer des berühmten Westweges schaffen, der von Pforzheim bis Basel führt. Alles übertrumpfend jedoch sind die Routen rings um den Feldberg, in dessen Nähe auch die Wiege des Skilaufs in Deutschland steht. Wer auf der Höhe bleiben möchte, kann über den Stübenwasen in sechs Stunden bis zum Belchen gelangen, diesem „Zauberberg", dem der Schönheitspreis zuerkannt werden muß. Man hat ihn auch „Balkon des Hochschwarzwaldes" genannt, weil er so souverän die Sicht über das Rheintal beherrscht. Jedenfalls hat keiner einen so wohlgeformten Charakterkopf wie der Belchen. Wer, statt zum Belchen zu wandern, am „Notschrei" auf halbem Weg nach Westen abbiegt, kommt über die „Halde" mit ihren vom Wind gebeutelten Buchen zum Schauinsland, dem Hausberg über der Freiburger Bucht.

Wo ein Berg ist, muß auch ein Tal sein. Das längste und eines der schönsten führt die „Wiese" hinunter, die Johann Peter Hebel „des Feldbergs liebliche Tochter" taufte. Den gleichen Weg geht es auch in den Hotzenwald, die einsamste und verwunschenste Ecke des Schwarzwaldes. Hier hausen die hartschädligen Hinterwälder, die vor keiner Obrigkeit kuschen. Vermutlich haben sie sich die benachbarten Eidgenossen zum Vorbild genommen. Jedenfalls werden herzerfrischende und zugleich traurige Geschichten von einigen Volksaufständen erzählt, bei denen sich die Hotzenwälder mit den Herren aus Wien angelegt haben, deren Statthalter lange Zeit dieses vorderösterreichische Land in Griff zu bekommen versuchten. Man nannte diese Händel „Salpeterkriege", weil der Rebellenführer der „Hotzen" ein Salpetersieder war, der sich bis zum Tod den Schneid nicht abkaufen ließ.

Der Hotzenwald zieht sich wie ein flaches Dach hinab bis zum Oberrhein zwischen Säckingen und Waldshut. Überall gibt es wundervolle „Zinken", beginnend beim Herzogenhorn bis hin zur hohen Mähr, die sich bereits der Schweizer Grenze nähert. In dieser urigen Landschaft findet man den Adlerfarn, die Wachholderheide oder die große Fetthenne, die sich mit ihrem knorrigen Holz auf den Gneisfelsen festkrallt. Auch hier sollte man sich daran erinnern, daß der ursprüngliche Baumbewuchs aus Buche und Eiche bestand. Erst später mußten die artenreichen Laubwälder den Tannenwäldern weichen. „Im Tal und auf der Höh", wie es im Lied heißt, liegen auch im Hotzenwald einige höchst sehenswerte Ortschaften. Allen voran St. Blasien in der Nähe des Schluchsees. Jeder Besucher reißt vor Verwunderung die Augen auf, wenn er die gewaltige Kuppel des Münsters vor sich sieht, die mit dem Petersdom in Rom zu wetteifern scheint.

Size before beauty. Not always, of course, but sometimes. Therefore anyone talking about the southern Black Forest has to start with the Feldberg. However, not only because at 1,493 metres (4,899 feet) high it puts all its rivals in the shade. It also dominates the whole mountain range as a result of its central location. This hump-backed giant is no ordinary mountain, but a "massif" which together with its satellites and offshoots casts its spell over the whole of the southern Black Forest. The Feldberg, bypassed by the Ice Age glaciers, is so massive and multifarious that one never forgets the sight of it. Everyone looking out for it as they approach from a distance can recognise it immediately by the wavy outline of its many hillocks. Even though its crest is marred by some ugly radar installations, it remains a magnet which frequently attracts hordes of people who turn up in their cars from all directions, but mainly from the Höllental.

Who is there to protect Nature from human beings, who makes sure that the bipeds keep to the signposted tracks? Recently it has been qualified rangers who see that everything is OK in the protected nature reserves. The idea comes from the "green sheriffs" in the USA. They make sure as far as possible that not all the flowers are picked and not all the meadows turned into nesting places for "highwaymen." If need be they resort to issuing a ticket, but usually leave it at a good-natured caution. In bureaucratic German these activities are known as "visitor guidance" or "gentle tourism."

Apart from a few "fairgrounds" the Black Forest remains a hikers' paradise. In all there are 22,000 kilometres (13,750 miles) of tracks, marked with lozenge-shaped signs and shown on maps. Anyone who is a good walker can—with or without a rucksack— cover the 270 kilometres (169 miles) of the famous western way from Pforzheim to Basle in 11 days. But they are all surpassed by the routes around the Feldberg, near the birthplace of skiing in Germany. Anyone wanting to stay up in the mountains can reach the "magic mountain" of Belchen in six hours via the Stubenwasen. This mountain must be awarded the prize for beauty. It has also been called the "Balcony of the High Black Forest" because of its commanding view over the Rhine Valley. In any case none of the mountains has a head which is as well-formed and full of character as the Belchen. If instead of climbing the Belchen you turn westwards en route at the "Notschrei" you will come, via the "Halde," with its beech trees bent over by the wind, to the vantage point of the Hausberg overlooking Freiburg.

Where there is a mountain, there must needs be a valley. The longest and one of the most beautiful leads down the meadow or "Wiese" which Johann Peter Hebel christened "the Feldberg's lovely daughter." This is also the way to the Hotzenwald, the most solitary and enchanted corner of the Black Forest. This is the home of the hard-headed Hinterwald people, who bow before no master. Presumably they have taken the neighbouring Swiss as their role model. Anyway, heart-warming and at the same time sad tales are told of popular rebellions when the Hotzenwalders came into conflict with the masters from Vienna, whose representatives long tried to gain the upper hand over this Austrian province. These events were known as "saltpetre wars" because the rebel leader of the "Hotzen" was a saltpetre boiler, who refused to yield until death.

The Hotzenwald slopes down like a flattish roof to the Upper Rhine between Säckingen and Waldshut. Everywhere there are wonderful mountain peaks, beginning with the Herzoghorn and reaching as far as the high Mähr not far from the Swiss border. In this primaeval landscape one finds eagle fern, dwarf juniper and the greater fat hen, its knotty wood clinging to the gneiss rocks. Here too one should remember that the original trees were beeches and oaks. Only later did the many kinds of deciduous trees have to give way to pine forests. "Up hill and down dale" the Hotzenwald too has some extremely attractive towns and villages, above all St Blasien near the Schluchsee. Every visitor's eyes open wide with amazement at the sight of the mighty dome of the minster, which seems to be competing with St Peter's in Rome.

La grandeur dispute à la beauté la prérogative du rang. Ce n'est certes pas toujours le cas, mais arrive, parfois. Qui se propose de parler de la Forêt-Noire se doit donc de commencer par le Feldberg. Car il ne fait pas qu'éclipser tous ses rivaux en raison de ses 1493 mètres d'altitude. Il domine également l'ensemble de cette chaîne de montagnes du fait de sa position centrale. Ce géant à l'échine arrondie n'est effectivement pas un sommet ordinaire, mais un «massif» sur l'orbite duquel gravitent des satellites et dont la force d'attraction s'exerce sur tout le sud de la Forêt-Noire. Le Feldberg auquel les champs de glace de l'époque glaciaire ont fait plier l'échine est si trapu et si nuancé d'aspect que sa vue se grave à jamais dans la mémoire. Tous ceux qui s'en approchent le cherchent des yeux, de loin déjà, le reconnaissant immédiatement à la crête ondulée que forment ses bosses. Et même si plusieurs installations de télécommunication plutôt rébarbatives ont envahi sa croupe, il n'a rien perdu du caractère d'aimant qu'il possède et qui certains jours, attire des foules de touristes, venus, dans leurs grosses limousines, de tous les azimuts, le plus souvent, toutefois, du Val d'Enfer.

Qui protège la nature de sa détérioration par l'homme, qui veille à ce que les bipèdes s'en tiennent aux sentiers balisés et aux pistes prévus à leur intention? Depuis un certain temps, ceci est de la compétence des «Rangers» qui viennent inspecter ces réserves naturelles. Leur action s'est inspirée des «shérifs verts» américains. Ils veillent, autant que faire se peut, à ce que toutes les fleurs ne soient pas arrachées et toutes les prairies transformées en «lieux de nidation» des «voleurs de grands chemins» de notre temps. Il vont même, à la rigueur, jusqu'à dresser des contraventions mais se contentent, la plupart du temps, de sermoner les fautifs. Dans le langage administratif, ces activités sont appelées «aiguillage du visiteur» ou «tourisme en douceur».

Mis à part les quelques endroits où se concentre le tourisme, la Forêt-Noire demeure le paradis des randonneurs. 22.000 kilomètres de sentiers de randonnée existent au total, tous balisés et indiqués sur les cartes topographiques. Le bon marcheur peut — avec ou sans sac-à-dos — parcourir en onze jours les 270 kilomètres de la célèbre «Route de l'Ouest» qui mène de Pforzheim à Bâle. Mais tout cela n'est rien à côté des itinéraires sillonnant le pourtour du Feldberg, sommet à proximité duquel fut pratiqué le ski pour la première fois en Allemagne. Celui qui préférera rester sur les hauteurs peut, en passant par le Stübenwasen, atteindre le Belchen en six heures de marche,» cette montagne magique» à qui le prix de beauté devrait être décerné. On l'a également dénom-

mée «le Balcon de la Haute Forêt-Noire» parce qu'il domine, en souverain, la vallée du Rhin. Toujours est-il qu'aucun autre sommet n'a une tête aussi bien faite et aussi typée que le Belchen. Ceux qui, arrivés à mi-chemin, au lieu-dit «Notschrei» (Cri de détresse), renoncent à faire l'ascension du Belchen et obliquent en direction de l'ouest, parviendront au «Schauinsland», le sommet surplombant la «baie de Fribourg» et le plus rapidement accessible pour les habitants de cette ville. Auparavant, ils auront traversé la «Halde», couverte de hêtres que le vent met à rude épreuve.

Qui dit montagne dit vallée. La plus longue et l'une des plus belles s'incline vers la plaine en longeant la Wiese, que Johann Peter Hebel baptisa «la douce fille du Feldberg». C'est par le même chemin que l'on entre dans le «Hotzenwald», la contrée boisée la plus retirée de la Forêt-Noire, et possédant le charme des régions restées à l'état vierge. C'est ici que «se terrent» les vrais hommes des bois à l'humeur cabocharde et rebelle que sont les habitants du Hotzenwald. Il est permis de supposer qu'ils ont pris exemple sur les Confédérés suisses, leurs voisins. Toujours est-il que des histoires plaisantes et tristes à la fois courent à ce sujet, relatant plusieurs soulèvements populaires qui opposèrent les habitants du Hotzenwald aux autorités viennoises qui, pendant longtemps, tentèrent de s'asujettir ce pays de «l'Autriche antérieure». On donna à ces démêlés le nom de «guerres du salpêtre», le meneur des rebelles étant un bouilleur de salpêtre qui, jusqu'à sa mort, refusa d'en rabattre.

Semblable à un toit plat incliné, le Hotzenwald s'étend jusqu'au Rhin supérieur, entre Säckingen et Waldshut. Partout pointent de merveilleuses «Dents», à commencer par celle de «Herzogshorn» en allant jusqu'à la «Mähr» de grande taille, déjà proche de la frontière suisse. Cette contrée restée à l'état originel est encore peuplée de fougères arborescentes, recouverte de landes où poussent le genévrier et la grande orpin qui s'accroche, de son bois noueux, à la roche gneissique. Là encore, il est bon de se rappeler qu'à l'origine, le boisement se constituait de hêtres et de chênes. Plus tard, les forêts à essences feuillues durent faire place aux sapins. Plusieurs bourgades tout particulièremnt dignes d'être visitées se blotissent dans les «vallées» et sur les «hauteurs» de la forêt Hotzenwald, comme on le dit dans la chanson. C'est en tout premier lieu Saint-Blasien, près du lac de Schluchsee. Le visiteur ne peut que s'émerveiller à la vue de l'énorme coupole de l'abbaye qui semble vouloir rivaliser avec la cathédrale Saint Pierre de Rome.

Auf halbem Weg der Berg-
straße zwischen Oberried
und Schauinsland zweigt
das kaum besiedelte Wil-
helmstal ab. Wer es durch-
wandert, hat fast pausenlos
den gewaltigen Buckel des
Feldberges im Blick. Man
muß allerdings ein guter
Wanderer sein, um die
mehr als tausend Meter
Höhenunterschied in
einem Anlauf zu schaffen.

The sparsely populated
Wilhelm Valley branches
off half-way along the
mountain road between
Oberried and Schauins-
land. Walking along it, you
have an almost uninter-
rupted view of the massive
hump of the Feldberg. Ad-
mittedly you need to be a
strong hiker to manage the
1,000 m (3,281ft) ascent in
one go.

C'est à mi-chemin de la
Bergstraße, entre Oberried
et Schauinsland, que bifurque la Wilhelmstal, vallée
où la population est très
clairsemée. Celui qui la
traversera à pied aura presque toujours l'énorme
échine du Feldberg dans
son champ visuel. Il est
toutefois nécessaire d'être
un bon randonneur pour
franchir les 1000 mètres de
dénivellation en une seule
fois.

Sommers ist der Titisee ein beliebter Tummel- und Rummelplatz für Bootsfahrer und Badelustige. Der gepflegte Kurort, der über das Höllental gut zu erreichen ist, liegt im Zentrum des Schwarzwaldes. Vom See aus hat man fast immer einen herrlichen Blick auf den Feldberg.

In summer, the Titisee is a popular gathering place for boaters and swimmers. The well-kept holiday resort, easily reached via the Höllental, is situated in the heart of the Black Forest. From the lake you almost always have a splendid view of the Feldberg.

En été, le lac Titisee est envahi par les amateurs de navigation de plaisance et les baigneurs. Cette coquette station climatique d'accès facile si l'on passe par le Val d'Enfer, se trouve au cœur de la Forêt-Noire. Du lac, on jouit presque toujours d'une vue splendide sur le Feldberg.

Die Landschaft um den Schluchsee gehört für viele Urlauber zu den begehrtesten im südlichen Schwarzwald. Ringsum gibt es endlose Wanderwege ohne allzu große Steigungen. Für den Wassersportler bietet der Schluchsee allerlei Abwechslung. Wie ruhig und einsam es hier sein kann, verrät die Morgenstimmung, die unser Fotograf in Schluchsee-Aule eingefangen hat.

For many holidaymakers the scenery around the Schluchsee is among the most desirable in the southern Black Forest. All around there are endless footpaths without any particularly steep ascents. Schluchsee also offers the water sports enthusiast all kinds of recreation. Just how peaceful and secluded it can be is reflected in the morning atmosphere as captured by our photographer in Schluchsee-Aule.

Beaucoup de vacanciers privilégient cette contrée entourant le lac Schluchsee, au sud de la Forêt-Noire. Cette région, qui n'est pas très accidentée, est sillonnée d'interminables sentiers de randonnée. L'amateur de sport nautique trouvera tout un éventail de possibilités au bord du lac de Schluchsee. L'atmosphère de sérénité, captée par notre photographe en cette heure matinale dans les bas-fonds du lac de Schluchsee laissent deviner combien le calme et la solitude peuvent y être profonds.

Wer eine echte alte Schwarzwaldmühle noch einmal kräftig klappern hören möchte, muß von St. Märgen aus zum „Hexenloch" hinabsteigen. Dort unten tief im Tal kann man sehen, wie erfindungsreich unsere Vorväter waren, als sie die Wasserkraft kostenlos zum Mahlen von Korn oder zum Sägen des Holzes zu nutzen wußten. Eine Besichtigung ist möglich.

Those who wish to hear a genuine old Black Forest mill clattering energetically must embark upon the climb down from St Märgen to the "Hexenloch" or "Witches' Hole". There, deep down in the valley, one can see how inventive our forefathers were, using water as a free source of energy to mill corn or to saw wood. The mill can be viewed by arrangement.

Qui serait désireux d'entendre encore une fois le claquement d'un vrai et vieux moulin de la Forêt-Noire descendra de St Märgen au «Hexenloch» (Trou aux Sorcières). Tout en bas, au plus profond du vallon, il pourra alors saisir ce que l'esprit inventif de nos ancêtres engendra, qui surent mettre gratuitement à profit la force hydraulique pour moudre le grain ou scier le bois. Il est possible d'en faire la visite.

Bad Säckingen ist eine traditionsreiche Stadt am Oberrhein. Kunsthistorisch bedeutsam ist das doppeltürmige Fridolinsmünster. Im Garten des Trompeterschlößchens (heute Heimatmuseum) wird die Geschichte des Trompeters von Säckingen wachgehalten, der — nach einem Versroman von Scheffel — ein hochwohlgeborenes Schloßfräulein umworben hat. Mit Erfolg!

Bad Säckingen on the Upper Rhine is a town steeped in tradition. The twin-towered minster of St Fridolin is of great artistic merit. The tale of the Trumpeter of Säckingen, who, according to a novel in verse by Scheffel, wooed and won a high-born lady of the castle, is kept alive in the garden of the "Trompeterschlösschen" or "Trumpeter's Castle," now a local history museum.

Bad Säckingen, située en bordure du Rhin supérieur, est une ville dont les origines remontent loin dans le passé. Du point de vue de l'histoire de l'art, le monastère Saint-Fridolin, qu'orne deux tours, revêt une importance particulière. Le Trompette de Säckingen et l'histoire qui se rattache à sa personne, furent immortalisés dans le «Trompeterschlößchen» (Châtelet du Trompette, aujourd'hui musée des arts locaux). Selon un roman en vers dû à Scheffel, ce trompette aurait fait une cour assidue à une jeune châtelaine de haute naissance, cour qui, selon toute apparence, ne demeura pas vaine.

Laufenburg liegt am Oberrhein, der aus der Schweiz kommend den Bodensee durchfließt und sich dann bis zur Nordsee durcharbeitet. Seine einmalige Lage unmittelbar am Flußrand macht Laufenburg zu einem beliebten Ausflugsziel. Früher war es ein bedeutender Handelsort für die Schifffahrt auf dem Rhein.

Laufenburg is on the upper Rhine, which flows from Switzerland through Lake Constance and makes its way right to the North Sea. Its unique location by the river makes Laufenburg a popular spot for visitors. It used to be an important trading centre for Rhine shipping.

Laufenburg est situé en bordure du cours supérieur du Rhin qui, né en Suisse, coule à travers le lac de Constance pour se frayer, ensuite, un chemin en direction de la Mer du Nord. Son site exceptionnel, sur les rives mêmes du fleuve, fait de Laufenburg un but d'excursions fort prisé. Autrefois place commerciale, cette ville joua un rôle important pour ce qui est de la navigation rhénane.

Wenn zwischen den deutschen Städten ein Schönheitswettbewerb veranstaltet würde, Freiburg wäre mit Sicherheit in der Spitzengruppe. Obwohl der Schwarzwald eine ganze Perlenkette geschlossener Ortschaften mit historischer Patina besitzt, kommt keine der „Breisgaumetropole" gleich. Sie ist das Herz- und Prunkstück der oberrheinischen Kulturlandschaft, fast so etwas wie ein Kultort für viele Fremde, die einmal in ihrem Leben den „schönsten Turm der Christenheit" sehen wollen. Das Münster zur Lieben Frau im Herzen der Stadt wird an Größe gewiß von anderen gotischen Bauwerken übertroffen, aber in seiner Klarheit und edlen Form besteht es jeden Vergleich. Seine Entstehung dankt es dem Glaubenseifer der Bürger, die dreihundert Jahre lang an ihrer Marien-Kirche gebaut haben. Sosehr sie ein ehrfurchtgebietendes Gotteshaus ist, so sehr ist sie zugleich ein vollkommenes Kunstwerk. Überwältigend vor allem das Ebenmaß des Turmes mit dem fast unmerklich geschwungenen Helm, der sich in die Weite des Horizonts zu recken scheint. Vom Glanz des Himmels wird er beleuchtet, sobald sich die Strahlen der untergehenden Sonne im Filigran seiner Kreuzblumen brechen und zu funkeln beginnen. Ebenso schön ist er auch in den Stunden der Nacht, wenn die Scheinwerfer seine schemenhafte Silhouette nachzeichnen.

Wie könnte man müde werden, den Liebreiz dieser Stadt zu bewundern, die eine alte Universität und den Sitz des gleichnamigen Erzbistums beherbergt. Sie ist über achthundert Jahre alt, nach dem Muster aller Zähringer-Städte kreuzförmig angelegt und mit zwei prächtigen Toren am Rande der alten Gemarkung versehen. Freiburg ist hochbetagt und wirkt doch jugendfrisch, durchzogen von einer Unzahl kleiner Bächlein, die aus dem Wasser der Dreisam abgezapft werden und dorthin wieder zurückfließen, sobald sie die Luft gereinigt und die Besu-

cher erfrischt haben. Das Gewirr der krummen Gäßchen, der Efeukranz der Berge, die Freiburg mit einem Wuschelkopf aus Bäumen schmücken, das Markttreiben auf dem Münsterplatz und das bunte Volk der vielen Studenten bestimmen die Atmosphäre. Hier, wo die Freiburger, auch „Bobbele" genannt, zu Hause sind, läßt sich's leben und in vielen versteckten Weinstuben wohl sein. Die Ausstrahlung Freiburgs reicht in sämtliche Himmelsrichtungen. Übers Höllental führen alle Wege (auch Eisenbahnen) ins Gebirge. Wer es ganz eilig hat, läßt sich von der Seilbahn auf den Schauinsland schaukeln. Oder er macht es wie jener Professor der Jurisprudenz, der in den frühen Morgenstunden regelmäßig den direkten Weg auf den Gipfel hinaufzujagen pflegte, ehe er frohgelaunt und gertenschlank sein Kolleg eröffnete.

In nächster Nähe von Freiburg liegen einige herrliche Schwarzwaldtäler. Die Krone gebührt dem Münstertal, das unablässig mit dem Anblick des Belchen lockt, den aber selbst ein „strammer" Wanderer frühestens nach fünf bis sechs Stunden erschöpft erreicht. An der Pforte zum Münstertal liegt Staufen, wo der Sage nach Faust zur Hölle gefahren sein soll, nachdem Mephisto ihm das Genick gebrochen hat. In nördlicher Richtung kommt man ins Glottertal, das durch die „Schwarzwaldklinik" zu Fernsehruhm gekommen ist, aber weitaus mehr seiner Sonnenlage, seines guten Essens und seiner Trachten wegen Aufmerksamkeit verdient. Noch ein paar Tips: das sonnendurchflutete Elztal und die heroische Landschaft des Simonwäldertales, das den Spuren der „wilden Gutach" bis zu den Kaskaden des Zweribaches folgt.

Der Breisgau hat aber noch mehr Superlative zu bieten. Am Kaiserstuhl, der sich bis nach Breisach direkt an die französische Grenze erstreckt, werden die höchsten Temperaturen Deutschlands gemessen. Dementsprechend „von der Sonne verwöhnt" ist der Wein, der auf lößhaltiger Vulkanerde gedeiht. Wen zum Durst auf belebenden Wein auch noch der Hunger auf köstliche Mahlzeiten überfällt, der kann fast in jedem Dorf entdecken, daß in dieser Insel der Seligen die beste ländliche Küche Deutschlands zu Hause ist. In den bürgerlichen Gasthöfen ist sie deftig, reichhaltig und preiswert. Aber natürlich findet auch der Schlemmer seine Luxusherbergen, an deren Tür die Sterne prangen, die vom französischen „Michelin" nach gnadenlos strengen Stichproben verliehen (oder gestrichen) werden. Wer sich im Konkurrenzkampf der Köche nicht von der französischen Cuisine inspirieren läßt, landet abgeschlagen am Tabellenende der gastronomischen Liga.

If there were to be a competition between German cities, Freiburg would without a doubt be among the front runners. Although the Black Forest has a whole chain of towns with their own historic aura, none of them is a match for the "Breisgau metropolis." It is the heart and showpiece of the Upper Rhine region and almost a cult place for many visitors, who want once in their lifetime to see the "loveliest tower in Christendom." Admittedly the Cathedral of Our Lady in the heart of the city is surpassed in size by other Gothic buildings, but in its nobility and clarity of form it can withstand any comparison. It owed its existence to the religious zeal of the town's citizens, who took 300 years to build their church to the Virgin Mary. It is as much a perfect work of art as an awe-inspiring house of the Lord. Most stunning of all is the elegantly proportioned tower with its almost imperceptibly curved helm roof, which seems to stretch far across the horizon. It is illuminated by the glow of heaven as soon as the rays of the setting sun break on the filigree of its finials and start to sparkle. But it is just as lovely at night when floodlights highlight its shadowy silhouette. How could one tire of admiring the charm of this city, which also houses an old university and the seat of the eponymous archbishop? It is over eight hundred years old and set out in a cruciform pattern like all Zähringer cities. It has two magnificent gates at the edge of the old town boundary. Freiburg is advanced in years and yet has the freshness of youth. It is crisscrossed by numerous streamlets which are drawn off from the waters of the River Dreisam and flow back into it after purifying the air and refreshing the visitors. The confusion of winding alleys, the ivy wreathe of the mountains whose trees seem to adorn Freiburg with a mop of curly hair, the hustle and bustle of the market on the cathedral square and the colourful appearance of the many students define the atmosphere. Here, in the home town of the "Bobbele", as the Freiburger is known in German, you can really live and feel at home in one of the many hidden wine bars.

Freiburg exudes its aura in all directions. All roads (and railways) across the Höllental lead into the mountains. Those who are in a hurry can ride by cable car up to the mountain-top viewpoint. Or they can follow the example of a certain professor of law who early each morning used regularly to run straight up the mountain before returning, happy and slim, to start his lectures.

Close by Freiburg there are some glorious Black Forest valleys. The gem among them is the Münster Valley with its unbroken view of the Belchen. However, even a hardened hiker will take at least five to six hours to reach it. At the entrance to the Münster Valley lies Staufen, where, according to legend, Faust is said to have descended into hell after Mephistopheles broke his neck. Northwards one comes upon the Glotter Valley, made famous by the TV series "Black Forest Clinic" but which deserves attention far more on account of its sunny location and traditional costumes. A few more tips: the sun-bathed Elz Valley and the heroic landscape of the Simonswald Valley, which follows the course of the "wild Gutach" as far as the Zweribach waterfalls.

However, the Breisgau region has yet more superlatives to offer. The highest temperatures in Germany are recorded on the Kaiserstuhl, which stretches right to Breisach right on the French border. The vines of the area, which flourish on volcanic soil containing loess, are accordingly "pampered" by the sun. Anyone overcome not only by thirst for invigorating wine but by hunger for delicious meals can discover in virtually every village that this "Isle of the Blessed" is home to the best country cooking in Germany. In the solid, respectable guest-houses it is substantial, rich and cheap. But the gourmet will of course also find luxury establishments with Michelin stars emblazoned on their doors, awarded (and removed) after mercilessly strict spot checks. In the world of competition between cooks, anyone not inspired by French cuisine ends up at the bottom of the league.

Si l'on organisait un concours de beauté parmi les villes allemandes, Fribourg se trouverait, à coup sûr, en tête du palmarès. Bien que la Forêt-Noire possède tout un chapelet d'agglomérations où l'Histoire a laissé sa patine, aucune ne peut se mesurer à la «Métropole du Brisgau». Elle est le coeur et le fleuron de la terre de civilisation allemande qu'est cette région du Rhin supérieur et, pour beaucoup d'étrangers, désireux de voir, une fois au moins dans leur vie, la «plus belle tour de la Chrétienté», elle va jusqu'à faire l'objet d'un véritable culte. La cathédrale «Zur lieben Frau», située en plein coeur de la ville, est certes dépassée en hauteur par d'autres édifices gothiques, mais, dans sa pureté et sa forme pleine de noblesse elle est en mesure de soutenir toute comparaison, quelle qu'elle soit. Elle doit d'avoir vu le jour à la ferveur des bourgeois de la ville qui, trois cents ans durant, ne cessèrent d'oeuvrer à l'édification de cette église vouée à la Vierge Marie. Vénérable Maison du Seigneur, elle est, en même temps, un chef d'oeuvre d'absolue perfection. Grandiose est, avant tout, l'harmonie des proportions de la tour dont la partie supérieure est incurvée de façon presque imperceptible et qui étire sa pointe dans le vaste espace de l'horizon. Le ciel la baigne de son éclat dès que les rayons du soleil couchant viennent se briser sur l'ajour de ses fleurons et que ceux-ci se mettent à étinceler. Mais sa beauté n'est en rien moindre aux heures de la nuit où les projecteurs font apparaître les contours de sa silhouette.

On ne saurait se lasser d'admirer le charme de cette ville qui abrite une vieille université et est, en même temps, le siège de l'archevêché du même nom. Elle a maintenant 800 ans et fut conçue sous forme de croix sur le modèle de toutes les villes fondées par les ducs de Zähringen, puis dotée de deux superbes portes situées en bordure de l'ancien territoire communal. Bien que la ville de Fribourg soit chargée d'ans, elle dégage une atmosphère de fraîcheur juvénile, parcourue qu'elle est d'une multitude de petits ruisseaux qui sont allés s'abreuver aux eaux de la Dreisam et y retournent dès qu'ils ont purifié l'air et rafraîchi le visiteur. Le dédale de ses ruelles tortueuses, les têtes bouclées des montagnes recouvertes d'arbres qui tressent une couronne à Fribourg, l'animation régnant sur la Place de la Cathédrale et la foule bigarrée des nombreux étudiants déterminent l'atmosphère qui lui est propre. Il fait bon vivre dans cette patrie des «Bobbele» (nom donné aux habitants de Fribourg), où l'on peut si agréablement s'attarder dans les nombreuses «Weinstuben» qui se cachent un peu partout.

Le rayonnement de Fribourg se déploie dans toutes les directions. Toutes les routes et voies ferroviaires menant en montagne passent par le Val d'Enfer. Le visiteur pressé se laissera transporter vers les hauteurs du «Schauinsland» au rythme cahoteux du téléférique. Ou il fera comme ce professeur de droit qui, à une heure matinale, avait coutume de gravir le sommet au pas de course par le chemin le plus court, avant de commencer, svelte et de bonne humeur, ses cours à l'université.

Dans les proches environs de Fribourg se situent plusieurs des merveilleuses vallées que possède la Forêt-Noire. La couronne revient à la Vallée de Münstertal qui attire en permanence les touristes en raison de la vue qui s'en dégage sur le Belchen, sommet que même le plus aguerri des randonneurs n'atteindra, éreinté, qu'après cinq ou six heures de marche. A l'entrée de la Vallée de Münstertal s'étend Staufen où, selon la légende, Faust descendit aux Enfers après que Méphisto lui eut brisé la nuque. En direction du nord, on parvient à la Vallée de Glottertal que le film «Schwarzwaldklinik», tourné à cet endroit, fit accéder au panthéon de la télévision, bien qu'elle mérite beaucoup plus l'attention du fait du site ensoleillé qu'elle occupe et des costumes traditionnels de ses habitants. Encore quelques petits «tuyaux»: la Vallée de l'Elz, inondée de soleil et le pays de légendes qu'est la vallée de Simonswald qui serpente en suivant les traces du «sauvage Gutach» et mène jusqu'aux cascades du «Zweribach».

Mais le Brisgau bat bien d'autres records. C'est au Kaiserstuhl, qui s'étend jusqu'à Vieux-Brisach, dans le voisinage direct de la frontière française que l'on enregistre les températures les plus élevées d'Allemagne. La vigne y est privilégiée par le soleil et pousse sur une terre volcanique contenant du loess. Et celui qui serait non seulement pris d'envie d'étancher sa soif en buvant un vin revigorant mais aimerait aussi assouvir sa faim en faisant un délicieux repas, découvrira, dans presque chaque village que ce pays de cocagne est également la patrie de la meilleure cuisine rustique d'Allemagne. Les auberges de campagne proposent une cuisine de type régional, copieuse et de prix modique. Mais les fines bouches y trouveront aussi des hostelleries de luxe, exhibant, à leurs portes, les étoiles qui leur ont été décernées (ou retirées) par le Guide Michelin, à l'issue de tests impitoyables. Ceux qui, dans la compétition que se livrent les cuisiniers, ne se laissent pas inspirer par l'art culinaire français, se retrouvent lanternes rouges de la ligue des gastronomes.

Keine Kirche im Schwarzwald ist so herrlich anzuschauen wie das Freiburger Münster mit seinem schlanken Turm. Im Untergeschoß des Hauptportals werden die Besucher von den „Klugen Jungfrauen" empfangen. Die mittelalterliche Bauhütte hat viele solcher vollendeter Skulpturen aus rotem Buntsandstein hervorgebracht.

No church in the Black Forest is as lovely to look at as Freiburg Cathedral with its slender tower. At the foot of the main door visitors are greeted by the "Wise Virgins". Mediaeval masons were responsible for many such accomplished red sandstone sculptures.

Aucune église, en Forêt-Noire, n'est aussi belle à contempler que la cathédrale de Fribourg que surmonte une tour élancée. A la partie inférieure du porche principal, les visiteurs sont accueillis par les «Vierges sages». De nombreuses autres sculptures du même degré de perfection sont issues de la loge maçonnique du Moyen Age.

Auf dem Freiburger Münsterplatz im Herzen der Stadt ist die ganze Woche über Markt. Er quillt über vor Obst und Gemüse, Blumen, Kräutern und Käse aus Frankreich. Wer beim Bummel von Durst geplagt wird, trinkt sein „Viertele" im berühmten „Oberkirch". Eine Augenweide ist die prächtige Häuserzeile rund um den Marktplatz. Von hier aus führen zahlreiche Gassen in alle Richtungen.

Every day is market day on the cathedral square in the heart of Freiburg. The market is a mass of fruit and vegetables, flowers, herbs and French cheeses. If looking around makes you thirsty, you can down a few "quarter litres" in the famous "Oberkirch." The superb rows of houses around the market square are a feast for the eyes. From here numerous alleys strike off in all directions.

Le marché se tient tous les jours de la semaine sur la Place de la Cathédrale de Fribourg, en plein cœur de la cité. Il regorge de fruits et de légumes, de fleurs, d'herbes aromatiques et de fromages français. Celui que la flânerie aura assoiffé, ira prendre son «Viertele», son quart de vin, dans le célèbre restaurant «Oberkirch». La rangée de splendides maisons bordant la Place du Marché est un régal pour les yeux. De nombreuses ruelles en divergent, menant dans toutes les directions.

Das Münstertal bei Staufen gilt vielen als das schönste Schwarzwaldtal und als Musterbeispiel einer offenen Landschaft. Es reckt sich mit seinen zahlreichen Seitentälern bis hoch hinauf auf den Belchen im Süden und den Schauinsland im Nordosten. Hier wird die Gastlichkeit großgeschrieben. Quartiere werden auch von manchen Bergbauern angeboten.

Many people consider the Münster Valley near Staufen to be the loveliest of all the Black Forest valleys and a perfect example of open countryside. Together with its numerous side-valleys, it stretches as far as the Belchen mountain in the South and the Schauinsland in the North-East. Here people set great store by hospitality. Many of the mountain farmers provide accommodation for visitors.

Nombreux sont ceux qui voient dans la Münstertal la plus belle des vallées de la Forêt-Noire et qui la considèrent comme un modèle de »paysage ouvert«. Dotée de nombreuses vallées transversales, elle ondule jusque sur les hauteurs du Belchen, au sud, et du Schauinsland, au nord-est. Une importance toute particulière est accordée à l'hospitalité par ses habitants et il est possible de trouver un gîte dans certaines fermes de montagne.

Das Markgräfliche Land im Süden von Freiburg bezaubert durch Sanftheit und Weite. Erst an den Rändern des südlichen Schwarzwaldes steigt die flache Rheinebene leicht an und sichert den Weinreben einen Platz an der Sonne. Hinter den Hügeln verstecken sich hübsche Dörfer und Städte, so wie hier Staufen hinter dem vulkanischen Kegel des Schloßberges (links).

The gentle open countryside of the Markgraf region south of Freiburg is captivating. Not until it reaches the edge of the southern Black Forest does the flat Rhine plain begin gradually to rise, thus providing the vines with a place in the sun. There are many pretty villages and towns tucked away behind the hills, such as Staufen, which lies behind the volcanic cone of the Schlossberg (left).

La région «Margräfliches Land», au sud de Fribourg, séduit le visiteur par sa douceur et la profondeur de son horizon. Ce n'est qu'aux confins de la Forêt-Noire, dans sa partie sud, que la plaine du Rhin commence à s'élever légèrement, permettant aux ceps de vigne de se faire une place au soleil. De jolis villages et villes se dissimulent derrière les collines comme ici, à Staufen, derrière les cônes volcaniques du Schloßberg (à gauche).

Der Kaiserstuhl ist die
wärmste Ecke Deutsch-
lands. Das bekommt dem
feurigen Wein, der auf vul-
kanischem Boden „von der
Sonne verwöhnt" wird. Die
gewaltige Reblandumbet-
tung hat zwar die Nutzung
der Anbaufläche erleich-
tert, doch auch manche
Kritik der „Traditionali-
sten" hervorgerufen. Die
Terrassierung ist ebenso
gut zu erkennen wie im
Hintergrund der Badberg
im Zentrum dieses frucht-
baren Vorgebirges.

The Kaiserstuhl is the
warmest place in Germany.
That suits the heady wine,
"spoiled by the sun" on the
volcanic soil. The terracing
of large areas of vineyard
has made it easier to make
full use of cultivable land,
but has also given rise to a
great deal of criticism from
"traditionalists." Here you
can clearly see the terraced
mountain slopes, and, in
the background, the
Badberg, rising amidst this
fertile foothill region.

Le Kaiserstuhl est la région
où sont mesurées les plus
hautes températures d'Allemagne. Cela profite au vin
généreux de cette contrée
qui pousse sur un sol volcanique et est «choyé par le
soleil». Le remembrement
des terres consacrées à la
culture de la vigne, pratiqué en grand style a,
certes, facilité l'exploitation
des vignobles, mais a également suscité de nombreuses critiques venant des
«traditionalistes». L'aménagement en terrasses est
aussi nettement discernable
que le Badberg qui se
dresse, à l'arrière-plan, au
beau milieu de ces fertiles
contreforts montagneux.

Die Erde ist mit Kunst übersät. Man muß sie nur aufspüren, man muß ihr Zeit und Liebe opfern. Die Kulturlandschaft des Schwarzwaldes jedenfalls läßt sich an einem Tag nicht erobern. Dafür sind die Kostbarkeiten zu weit verstreut, in abgelegenen Winkeln und Tälern versteckt, oder sie sitzen weitab auf der Höhe, wo man nur Wälder vermutet, aber keine Kirchen und Klöster. Kaum je ist das Wort von der Kulturlandschaft angemessener. Denn die Urbarmachung des Schwarzwaldes, seine Erschließung (und damit auch Christianisierung) war das große Werk der mittelalterlichen Reformorden: der Benediktiner, der Cluniazenser, der Zisterzienser. Das geschah im 7. Jahrhundert und vollzog sich in drei Schüben. Zuerst drangen einzelne Mönche in das Gebirge vor, danach bildeten sich kleine Gemeinschaften, zuletzt schließlich erfolgten die Klostergründungen. Ihre Devise hieß: Askese, Zucht und Armut. Diese Klöster haben nicht nur geistliche, sondern auch „weltliche" Grundherrschaften, also richtige Kleinstaaten, gegründet. Natürlich gibt es auch zahlreiche Dokumente aus frühgeschichtlicher Zeit, altgermanische Opfersteine und Hügelgräber, aber erst mit den christlichen Bauwerken kommt gleichsam Licht in das Dunkel der ehedem so unzugänglichen Wälder. Nun erst beginnt die Rodung und die Fruchtbarmachung der Felder.

Das erste und noch heute imposanteste Kloster ist St. Trudpert im Münstertal, das als rechtsrheinisches Benediktinerkloster entstand, später barockisiert wurde und schließlich der Säkularisation anheimfiel. Kirche und Kloster lassen die Handschrift des Vorarlberger Barockbaumeisters Peter Thumb erkennen, dem ungewöhnlich viele Sakralbauten im Schwarzwald zu danken sind, darunter die im benachbarten St. Ulrich und im versteckten Ettenheimmünster zwischen Emmendingen und Lahr.

Thumbs Meisterwerk im Schwarzwald ist St. Peter, hoch über dem Glottertal gelegen, mit weitem Rundblick auf die wellige Hügellandschaft zwischen Kandel und Feldberg. Was soll man mehr bewundern? Die klar gegliederte Sandsteinfassade der Kirche, den Reichtum des Innenraums mit seinem grandiosen Orgelprospekt, die souveräne Lage der Klosteranlage, die heute das Priesterseminar der Diözese Freiburg beherbergt, oder das Rokoko-Juwel der Klosterbibliothek im Obergeschoß des Konviktbaus? Wer Peter Thumb nennt, muß wenigstens die Stadtkirche von Waldkirch erwähnen, die Ruine von Frauenalb im Nordschwarzwald, und nicht · zu vergessen: Birnau am Bodensee, in dem das südwestdeutsche Spätbarock seinen krönenden Abschluß findet.

In den frühen Jahrhunderten, das wird von uns Spätgeborenen oft vergessen, gab es noch keine politischen oder nationalstaatlichen Grenzen. Der oberrheinische Kulturraum war nach allen Seiten offen. Die entscheidenden Impulse erhielt er von Frankreich, von dorther kam aber zur Zeit Ludwig XIV. die Bedrohung, die mit der Zerstörung des Heidelberger Schlosses das größte Brandmal hinterließ. Erst heute wächst die „Regio" wieder zusammen, ohne daß die „Durchlässigkeit", die Europa schon einmal besessen hat, schon wieder erreicht wäre.

Oft war der Rhein eine blutende Grenze. Man spürt es in Breisach, wo Furt und Feste beieinander liegen. Oben auf dem felsigen Burgberg thront das Stephans-Münster, an dem sich von der Romanik bis zum Barock alle Stilarten ablesen lassen. Im Innern befinden sich ein grandioses Fresko von Martin Schongauer und der spätgotische Schnitzaltar eines anonymen Meisters. Breisach erinnert daran, daß es in allen Epochen einschneidende, aber auch produktive Wechselwirkungen gegeben hat. Eine der erstaunlichsten ist St. Blasien, dessen Kuppel mit 64 Meter Höhe als drittgrößte Europas gilt. Gebaut hat sie d'Ixnard, der aus dem nahen Straßburg kam und den frühen Klassizismus repräsentiert. Aber auch diese Abtei (heute Jesuiteninternat) ist in Wahrheit schon über tausend Jahre alt und von reicher Geschichte.

So ist das mit der Kultur. Sie ist zu vielschichtig, um ihre wichtigsten Monumente auch nur erwähnen zu können. Viele Seiten müßte man den wunderbaren Städten widmen, die in Jahrhunderten gewachsen sind, den zahllosen Ruinen, die als stumme Zeugen der Geschichte in unsere Zeit ragen und nicht zuletzt den monumentalen Überresten aus der romanischen Epoche, die in Hirsau und Alpirsbach zu bewundern sind.

Wo immer wir Station machen, wir berühren eine europäische Pulsader. Das Elsaß ist zum Greifen nahe. Dort sprechen viele (mehr insgeheim als offiziell) ein kerniges „Elsäßerdütsch". Trotzdem sind wir in Frankreich, und man spürt schon die Nähe von Paris. Das romanische Burgund liegt vor der Haustür, zum Mittelmeer kann man in einem halben Tag gelangen, die Schweiz befindet sich gleich um die Ecke. Wer da nicht ins Schwärmen gerät, der hat keine Augen im Kopf.

The Earth is strewn with art. You just have to seek it out, and sacrifice time and devotion to it. The man-made landscape of the Black Forest, in any case, can't be managed in a day. The treasures are too widely scattered, hidden away in secluded corners and valleys or way up on the heights where you would think there were only trees, not churches or monasteries. There could hardly ever be a more appropriate use of the term "man-made landscape." For the initial clearing of the Black Forest, its opening up (accompanied by its conversion to Christianity) was the great achievement of the mediaeval reform orders of the Benedictines, Cluniacs and Cistercians. This took place in the seventh century AD and was completed in three phases. First individual monks advanced into the mountains, followed by the formation of small communities, and finally by the founding of the monasteries. Their motto was: asceticism, discipline and poverty. These monasteries founded not only religious but also secular manorial communities which were small towns in their own right. Of course there are also numerous early historic documents, old Germanic sacrificial stones and tumuli. But only with the coming of the Christian edifices did light so to speak penetrate the darkness of these inaccessible forests. Only then were the clearings begun and the fields reclaimed.

The first of the monasteries, still imposing today, is St Trudpert in the Münster Valley, the Benedictine monastery on the right bank of the Rhine, which was later transformed in the Baroque style and finally fell victim to secularisation. Both church and monastery bear the mark of Peter Thumb, the Baroque master builder from Vorarlberg, to whom we owe an extraordinary number of sacred buildings in the Black Forest, in neighbouring St Ulrich and secluded Ettenheimmünster, tucked away between Emmendingen and Lahr.

Thumb's Black Forest masterpiece is St Peter's, lying high above the Glotter Valley, with a view in all directions across the undulating highland landscape between Kandel and Feldberg. What should one admire more? The clear lines of the church's sandstone facade, the richness of the interior with its grandiose organ backdrop, the commanding location of the monastery complex, which nowadays houses the seminary of the Diocese of Freiburg, or the Rococo gem of the monastery library on the upper floor of the seminary building? Anyone speaking of Peter Thumb must at least mention the parish church in Waldkirch and the ruins of Frauenalb in the northern Black Forest, not forgetting Birnau on Lake Constance, the culmination of south-west German late Baroque.

Those of us born later often forget that in the early centuries there were no political or national state borders. As a cultural area the Upper Rhine was open on all sides. It received its decisive inspiration from France. During the reign of Louis XIV the threat came from that side too, leaving behind it the tremendous scar of the destruction of Heidelberg Castle. Only nowadays is the region growing closer together again, without having reached the level of permeability which Europe once possessed.

The Rhine was often a bloody border. You sense it in Breisach, where ford and fortress lie beside each other. High up on the craggy Burgberg stands the Cathedral of St Stephan, demonstrating all architectural styles from Romanesque to Baroque. Inside there is a grandiose fresco by Martin Schongauer and the late Gothic carved altar by an unknown master. Breisach reminds one that in all epochs there were far-reaching, but also productive, interactions. One of the most astonishing is St Blasien, whose 64-metre (210-foot) dome is the third tallest in Europe. It was built by d'Ixnard, who came from nearby Strasbourg and represents early classicism. But this abbey too (nowadays a Jesuit boarding school) is in fact already over 1,000 years old and has a colourful history.

So much for culture. It is too multi-layered even to mention only its most important monuments. One ought to devote many pages to the wonderful towns and cities which have grown up over centuries, the innumerable ruins towering as silent witnesses to history in our time, and not least to the monumental remains of the Romanesque epoch which one can admire in Hirsau and Alpirsbach.

Wherever we decide to break our journey, we shall touch on one of the arteries of Europe. Alsace is a stone's throw away. There many people (more in private than officially) speak a pithy "Alsatian German." Nevertheless, they are in France and one can already sense the proximity of Paris. Romanesque Burgundy is at your door. You can reach the Mediterranean in half a day. Switzerland is just round the corner. If all this isn't enough to move you, you simply don't have eyes to see.

La terre est parsemée d'œuvres d'art. Il n'est que d'aller à leur découverte et de leur sacrifier du temps. La terre de civilisation que représente la Forêt-Noire ne peut être conquise en un seul jour. En effet, les merveilles dont elle abonde sont disséminées dans le paysage, cachées dans les recoins et les vallées ou dissimulées sur les hauteurs. Jamais le terme de «terre de civilisation» n'a été plus exact. En effet, le défrichage et la mise en valeur de la Forêt-Noire (de même que sa christianisation) fut l'œuvre éminente des ordres de l'Eglise réformée: Bénédictins, Clunisiens, Cisterciens. Ceci se passait au septième siècle et se déroula en trois temps. Des moines apparurent tout d'abord isolément et pénétrèrent au cœur de cette chaîne de montagnes, puis de petites communautés se constituèrent qui finirent par fonder des monastères. Leur devise: ascétisme, discipline et dénuement. Il est bien évident qu'on y trouve également de nombreux témoignages de la période protohistorique, tels que lieux de sacrifice et tumulus datant d'avant notre ère, mais ce n'est qu'avec les édifices chrétiens que la lumière se fit et vint éclairer l'obscurité de ces forêts jadis impénétrables. C'est alors seulement que commence le défrichement et la fertilisation des champs.

Le plus imposant des monastères est, aujourd'hui encore celui de St Trudpert, dans la vallée de la Münster qui fut le premier de l'ordre des Bénédictins à voir le jour sur la rive droite du Rhin, monastère qui fut remanié, par la suite, dans le style baroque et finit par être sécularisé. L'église et le monastère trahissent le style de leur architecte, Peter Thumb, originaire du Voralberg et artiste du baroque, à qui l'on doit un nombre surprenant d'édifices religieux, comme par exemple ceux que l'on peut voir à St. Ulrich ou dans la bourgade de Ettenheimmünster qui se cache entre Emmendingen et Lahr.

Le chef d'œuvre de Thumb en Forêt-Noire est l'église St Pierre, dominant la vallée de la Glotter et offrant une vue circulaire sur le paysage mamelonné qui s'étend entre le Kandel et le Feldberg Que doit-on admirer le plus? La façade de grès rouge de l'église, à la disposition rigoureuse, l'opulence de l'intérieur avec ses orgues grandioses, ou la position dominante de l'ensemble du monastère qui abrite aujourd'hui ce joyau de la période rococo qu'est la bibliothèque du monastère. Celui qui prononce le nom de Peter Thumb devra au moins mentionner l'église de la ville de Waldkirch, les ruines de Frauenalb, dans le nord de la Forêt-Noire et ne saurait oublier Birnau, sur les rives du lac de Constance, où triomphe le baroque tardif, caractéristique du sud de l'Allemagne.

Au cours des siècles passés, — c'est ce que nous, qui sommes nés sur le tard dans notre millénaire, avons tendance à oublier —, les frontières politiques ou nationales n'existaient pas. L'aire de civilisation que représente la région du Rhin supérieur était ouverte à tous les vents. Les impulsions maîtresses lui vinrent de France, mais c'est de là que, à l'époque de Louis XIV, surgit aussi la menace qui se traduisit ensuite par la destruction du château de Heidelberg et laissa de profonds stigmates. Il aura fallu attendre les temps présents pour que cette région commence à se ressouder, sans toutefois que la perméabilité que l'Europe a jadis possédé ait pu, de nouveau, se faire jour.

Souvent, au cours de l'Histoire, le Rhin a été une frontière où s'est épanché le sang. On en prend conscience à Vieux-Brisach où le guet et la forteresse se côtoient. Sur les hauteurs rocheuses du Burgberg trône la cathédrale St Stéphane qui trahit les différents styles ayant présidé à sa construction, styles qui vont du roman au baroque. A l'intérieur, on admirera une fresque grandiose dont Martin Schongauer est l'auteur ainsi que le maître-autel sculpté datant du gothique tardif, œuvre d'un maître inconnu. Vieux-Brisach nous rappelle qu'il y eut, à toutes les époques, des interactions aux incidences fondamentales mais aussi positives. Symbolisant ce phénomène, l'église St Blasien, dont la coupole atteignant 65 mètres en fait la troisième d'Europe, en est l'un des exemples les plus surprenants. Elle fut érigée par d'Ixnard, originaire de Strasbourg, la ville voisine, et représente le clacissisme à ses débuts.

Ainsi en est-il de la civilisation. Elle est trop complexe pour que l'on puisse en dégager les monuments même les plus importants. Il faudrait consacrer de nombreuses pages à ces merveilleuses villes qui ont pris forme au cours des siècles, aux ruines innombrables, témoins muets se dressant encore de nos jours, sans oublier les vestiges monumentaux de l'époqe romantique que l'on peut admirer à Hirsau et à Alpirsbach.

Ou que nous nous arrêtions, c'est une artère radiale de l'Europe que nous effleurons. L'Alsace est à portée de la main. Beaucoup y parlent (plus sous le manteau qu'officiellement) un dialecte alsacien d'origine germanique haut en couleur. Et pourtant, on est en France, et l'on sent déjà la proximité de Paris. La Bourgogne romane est toute proche, la Méditerranée n'est qu'à une demi-journée de route, la Suisse, à côté. Ne pas s'exalter à la vue de cette région, c'est être décidément frappé de cécité.

St. Trudpert, die erste
rechtsrheinische Benedikti-
nergründung, ist von dem
Vorarlberger Baumeister
Peter Thumb glanzvoll
barockisiert worden. Be-
sonders prachtvoll ist das
Kircheninnere. Die Lage
des mächtigen Klosters auf
halber Höhe in der weiten
Talaue ist überwältigend.

St Trudpert, the first
Benedictine monastery on
the right bank of the
Rhine, was transformed in
dazzling Baroque style by
Peter Thumb, the famous
master-builder from
Vorarlberg in Austria. The
church interior is par-
ticularly magnificent.
Situated as it is half-way
up a hillside overlooking
the sweeping water
meadows, the mighty
monastery is a truly imposing sight.

Saint Trudpert, le premier
monastère à avoir été fondé
par les Bénédictins sur la
rive droite du Rhin fut
splendidement remanié
dans le style baroque par
Peter Thumb, bâtisseur
originaire du Voralberg.
On admirera l'intérieur
somptueux de l'église. Cet
imposant monastère, situé
à mi-hauteur de la colline,
dans une vallée évasée, est
absolument grandiose.

Das Stephansmünster in
Breisach liegt eindrucksvoll
auf einer kleinen Anhöhe
direkt am Rheinufer, wo
die Brücke nach Frank-
reich führt. Die „strategi-
sche Lage" an der Grenze
hat die Geschichte des idyl-
lischen Städtchens be-
stimmt. Es wird beherrscht
von der wuchtigen Kirche,
die ein Kompendium der
Baugeschichte darstellt. Im
Innern ein bedeutendes
Fresko von Schongauer
und ein schöner Schnitz-
altar.

St Stephan's cathedral in
Breisach is impressively
situated on a small hillock
right on the bank of the
Rhine where the bridge
crosses over into France.
This "strategic" border
location has determined
the history of this idyllic
little town. It is dominated
by the grandiose church,
which demonstrates a com-
pendium of architectural
history. The interior contains an important fresco
by Schongauer and a
beautiful carved altar.

La cathédrale St Stéphane
à Vieux-Brisach dresse sa
silhouette imposante sur
une butte tout près de la
rive du Rhin, là où le pont
mène vers la France. L'histoire de cette petite ville
d'aspect idyllique a été
déterminée par la «position
stratégique» qu'elle occupe,
à proximité directe de la
frontière. Elle est dominée
par son église trapue qui
représente un abrégé de
l'histoire des styles archi-
tecturaux. A l'intérieur, on
admirera l'importante fresque exécutée par Schon-
gauer et un beau maître-
autel sculpté.

Die Klosterkirche von St. Blasien mit ihrer gewaltigen Kuppel ist eines der Bauwunder im südlichen Schwarzwald. Das frühklassizistische Kloster nahe beim Schluchsee entstand Ende des 18. Jahrhunderts über altem Baugrund. Heute beherbergt es ein von Jesuitenpatres geleitetes Gymnasium mit Internat. Ein Platz für Meditation und Erholung.

The monastery church of St Blasien with its mighty dome is one of the architectural wonders of the southern Black Forest. The Early Classical monastery by the Schluchsee was built towards the end of the 18th century on the site of an earlier building. Nowadays it houses a boarding school run by Jesuit priests. A place for meditation and recuperation.

L'église du monastère Saint Blasien, surmontée d'une énorme coupole, est l'une des merveilles architecturales du sud de la Forêt-Noire. Ce monastère, datant des débuts de la période néo-classique et situé près du lac de Schluchsee fut érigé au XVIIIe siècle sur des fondements déjà existants. Il abrite aujourd'hui un lycée et un internat dirigés par des pères jésuites. Tout y invite à la méditation et à la détente.

St. Peter liegt am Ausgang
des Glottertals mit Blick
auf die wellenförmige
Landschaft bis hin zum
Feldberg. Besonders ein-
drucksvoll ist die Klosteranlage. Neben der Kirche
sollte man in keinem Fall
den Besuch der
Klosterbibliothek versäu-
men, die zu Recht als
schönster Rokokoraum im
Breisgau gilt. Die Besuchs-
zeiten sollte man jedoch
bei der Kurverwaltung er-
fragen.

St Peter's is at the end of
the Glotter Valley and
enjoys a view across the
undulating countryside as
far as Feldberg. The
monastery complex is par-
ticularly impressive. In addition to the church, you
shouldn't miss paying a
visit to the monastery
library, justifiably con-
sidered to be the most
beautiful Rococo room in
the Breisgau region. Be
sure to check the visiting
hours with the local tourist
office.

St Peter se trouve à l'issue
de la Glottertal. Il s'en
dégage une vue plongeante
sur le relief mamelonné des
alentours, s'étendant
jusqu'au Feldberg.
L'ensemble des bâtiments
conventuels est d'une
impressionnante majesté.
On ne manquera de visiter
ni l'église ni, en particulier,
la bibliothèque qui, à juste
titre, passe pour être la
plus belle pièce baroque du
Brisgau. Il est toutefois
recommandé de s'informer
auprès de l'office de la station climatique des heures
d'ouverture.

Hirsau war der Ausgangspunkt der cluniazensischen Reformbewegung auf deutschem Boden. Dieser sehenswerte Ort im oberen Nagoldtal birgt zahlreiche historische Bauten: Teile des romanischen Langhauses, einen Kreuzgang aus dem 15. Jahrhundert, den „Eulenturm" und imposante Renaissance-Ruinen des ausgebrannten Jagdschlosses der württembergischen Herzöge.

Hirsau was the starting point for the Cluniac reform movement in Germany. This picturesque town in the upper Nagold Valley contains many historic buildings, including the remains of a Roman longhouse, a 15th-century cloister, the "Eulenturm" or "Owl Tower" and the majestic Renaissance ruins of a burnt-out hunting lodge belonging to the Dukes of Württemberg.

Hirsau fut, sur le sol allemand, le point de départ du mouvement de réforme de l'ordre clunisien. Cette remarquable localité, située en amont de la Nagold, dans la vallée du même nom, recèle de nombreux bâtiments historiques: les vestiges de la nef romane, le cloître remontant au XVe siècle, la «Eulenturm» (Tour des Chats-Huants) et les ruines imposantes de style Renaissance du château de chasse qui appartint aux ducs de Wurtemberg et fut entièrement détruit par un incendie.

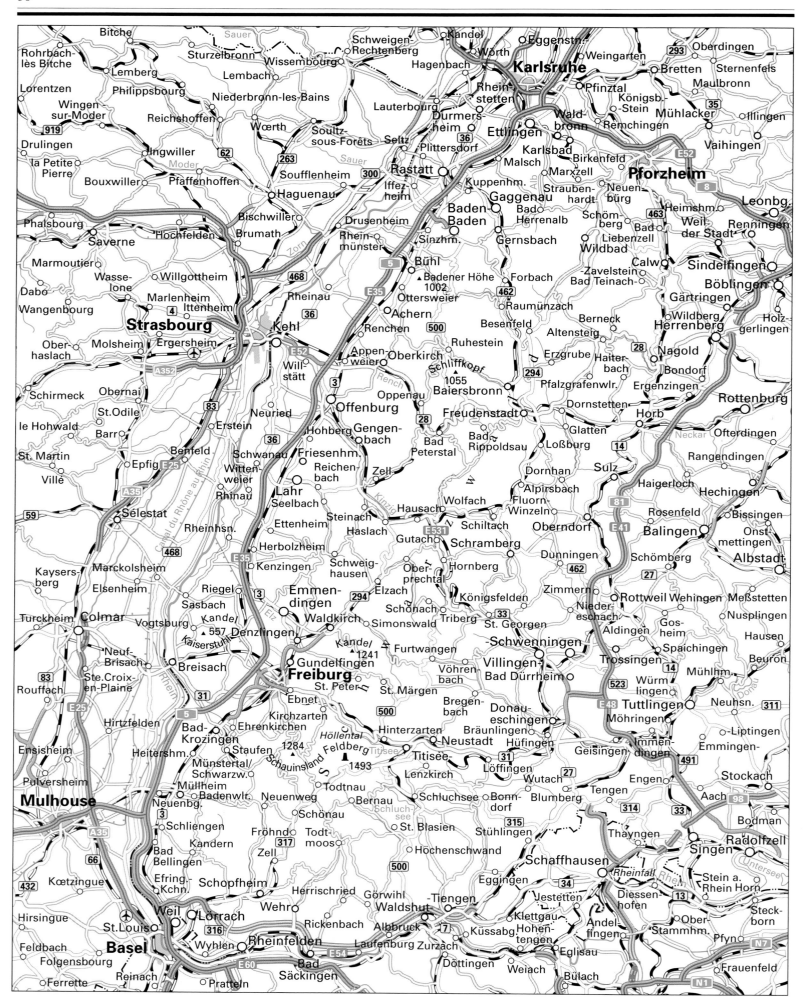